Prentice Hall LITERATURE

PENGUIN EDITION

Unit Five
Resources

Grade Seven

PEARSON

Upper Saddle River, New Jersey
Boston, Massachusetts
Chandler, Arizona
Glenview, Illinois
Shoreview, Minnesota

BQ Tunes Credits

Keith London, Defi ned Mind, Inc., Executive Producer
Mike Pandolfo, Wonderful, Producer
All songs mixed and mastered by Mike Pandolfo, Wonderful
Vlad Gutkovich, Wonderful, Assistant Engineer
Recorded November 2007 – February 2008 in SoHo, New York City, at
Wonderful, 594 Broadway

13-digit ISBN: 978-0-13-366440-9
10-digit ISBN: 0-13-366440-6

1 2 3 4 5 6 7 8 9 10   12 11 10 9 8

CONTENTS

For information about the Unit Resources, assessing fluency, and teaching with BQ Tunes, see the opening pages of your Unit One Resources.

from **A Christmas Carol: Scrooge and Marley,** *Act I*, **Scenes 2 and 5,**
by Israel Horovitz

Writing Workshop: Research—Multimedia Report **82**

Writing Workshop: Common Usage Problems **83**

Benchmark Test 9 . . . . **84**

Skills Concept Map 2 . . . . **90**

"The Monsters Are Due on Maple Street" by Rod Serling

True Identity, performed by Carolyn Sills and the Boss Tweed Band

People make **assumptions**, think their opinion must be true,

that your **image**, or how you present yourself, is the actual you.

So if you think that their opinion is **biased** or personally skewed,

just be yourself so they can rightfully **define** and describe you.

You can't **ignore**, or not acknowledge, who you are.

Your looks and your **appearance** will only take you so far.

So **appreciate** and be grateful for what makes you one of a kind

and show the world, reveal to them, what's really on your mind

Your **reaction** or response to life's daily ins and outs

is all some people need to think they know what you're all about.

So if you want to **reflect** or show how you truly are inside,

make use of your features and characteristics, to imitate is simply to hide.

You can't **ignore**, or not acknowledge, who you are.

Your looks and **appearance** will only take you so far.

So **appreciate** and be grateful for what makes you one of a kind

and show the world, reveal to them, what's really on your mind

How other people see things, **perceptions**, can hold true

if you refuse to concentrate or focus on the real you.

So if you think they have the wrong **perspective** or point of view,

Just make sure that your identity, your true self, is shining through.

You can't **ignore**, or not acknowledge, who you are.

Your looks and **appearance** will only take you so far.

So **appreciate** and be grateful for what makes you one of a kind

and show the world, **reveal** to them, what's really on your mind

and show the world, **reveal** to them, what's really on your mind

and show the world, **reveal** to them, what's really on your mind

Continued

Song Title: **True Identity**
Artist / Performed by Carolyn Sills and the Boss Tweed Band
Vocals & Bass Guitar: Carolyn Sills
Guitar: Gerard Egan
Drums: Vlad Gutkovich
Lyrics by Carolyn Sills
Music composed by Carolyn Sills & the Boss Tweed Band

Name _____ Date _____

Unit 5: Drama
Big Question Vocabulary—1

The Big Question: Do others really see us?

appreciate: *v.* to understand something's importance or value; other form: *appreciation*

assumption: *n.* a decision that something is true, without definite proof; other form: *assume*

bias: *n.* the act of favoring one group of people over another; other form: *biased*

define: *v.* to describe something correctly and thoroughly; other forms: *definition, defined*

reveal: *v.* to expose something that has been hidden or secret; other forms: *revealed, revealing*

A. DIRECTIONS: *In the chart, write a synonym and an antonym for each vocabulary word. Choose your answers from the words and phrases in the box. You will not use all of them.*

| theory | fairness | distort | be thankful | be happy | be ungrateful | hide |
| characterize | uncover | proof | pride | concentrate | prejudice | |

Word	Synonym	Antonym
1. appreciate		
2. assumption		
3. bias		
4. define		
5. reveal		

B. DIRECTIONS: *Write a humorous short story about a man who receives a large parrot for a pet. At first he is unhappy because he doesn't like birds. However, the parrot is so clever that the man changes his mind. Use all five vocabulary words.*

_____

_____

_____

_____

_____

_____

Name _____ Date _____

Unit 5: Drama
Big Question Vocabulary—2

The Big Question: Do others really see us?

appearance: *n.* the way a person looks to other people; other forms: *appear, appearing*

focus: *v.* to direct one's attention to one specific thing; other forms: *focusing, focused*

identify: *v.* to recognize and correctly name something; other forms: *identification, identified*

ignore: *v.* to act as if something has not been seen or heard; other forms: *ignoring, ignorant*

perspective: *n.* a special way to think about something, usually influenced by one's personality and experiences

A. DIRECTIONS: *Write the vocabulary word that best completes each group of related words.*

1. avoid, neglect, forget, _____

2. attitude, viewpoint, thoughts, _____

3. looks, image, personality, _____

4. concentrate, stare, study, _____

5. classify, define, describe, _____

B. DIRECTIONS: *On the line before each sentence, write* True *if the statement is true, or* False *if it is false. If the statement is false, rewrite the sentence so that it is true.*

_____1. A person's *appearance* is his or her innermost thoughts.

_____

_____2. If the fire alarm goes off, the best course of action is to *ignore* it.

_____

_____3. To board an airplane, you must carry a suitcase in order to *identify* yourself.

_____

_____4. Activities that require you to *focus* carefully include sleeping and daydreaming.

_____

_____5. A person's *perspective* is often based on opinions and attitudes.

_____

Name _____ Date _____

Unit 5: Drama
Big Question Vocabulary—3

The Big Question: Do others really see us?

characteristic: *n.* a special quality or feature that is typical of someone or something

image: *n.* the way a person appears to others; other forms: *images, imagination, imagine*

perception: *n.* the unique way you think about someone or something; other form: *perceive*

reaction: *n.* a response to someone or something in the form of thoughts, words, or actions; other forms: *react, reactionary*

reflect: *v.* to express or show through gestures or actions; other forms: *reflection, reflected*

Karen said this to Mario, Heidi, and Ramon: "I saw a really strange looking man on the subway. He gave me a spooky feeling. Maybe he was a magician. Anyway, he was carrying a huge bag. I peeked inside and almost fainted with shock. It was a painting—a painting of ME!"

Each of Karen's friends had a different reaction to what she said.

DIRECTIONS: *Use the word(s) shown to write what each friend said to Karen.*

characteristic(s), image

Mario

perception

Heidi

reflect, reaction

Ramon

Name _____ Date _____

Unit 5: Drama
Applying the Big Question

Do others see us more clearly than we see ourselves?

DIRECTIONS: *Complete the chart below to apply what you have learned about how people form impressions of others. One row has been completed for you.*

Example	Who/What is Judged	Who does the Judging	Is the judgment fair	What I learned
From Literature	Goodman in "The Monsters . . .	His neighbors	No, it is based on the fact that he is an "oddball"	Fear can change the way people see others
From Literature				
From Science				
From Social Studies				
From Real Life				

Name _____

Unit 5: Drama Skills Concept Map—1

Do others see us more clearly than we see ourselves?

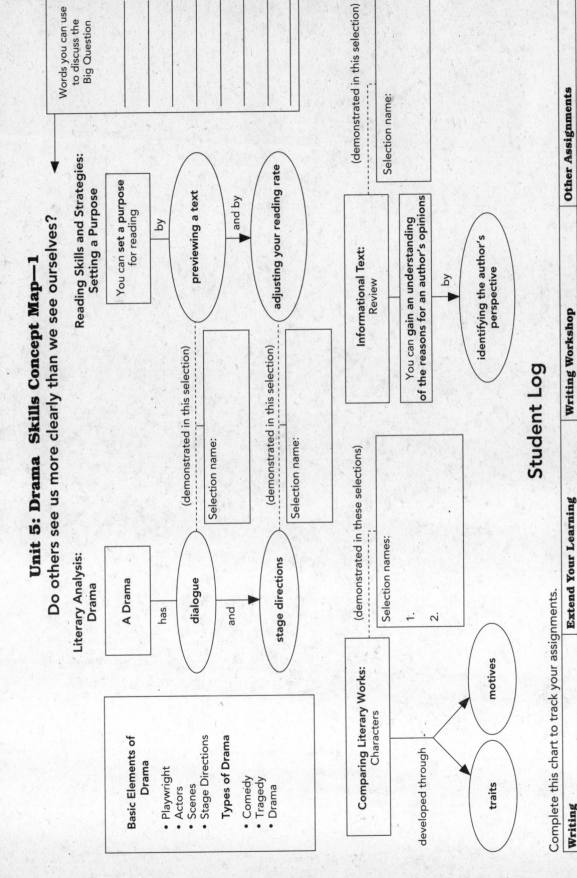

Literary Analysis:
Drama

Words you can use to discuss the Big Question

Reading Skills and Strategies:
Setting a Purpose

You can set a purpose for reading

by

previewing a text

and by

adjusting your reading rate

(demonstrated in this selection)

Selection name:

Informational Text:
Review

You can gain an understanding of the reasons for an author's opinions

by

identifying the author's perspective

(demonstrated in this selection)

Selection name:

A Drama

has

dialogue

and

stage directions

(demonstrated in this selection)

Selection name:

(demonstrated in this selection)

Selection name:

Basic Elements of Drama
- Playwright
- Actors
- Scenes
- Stage Directions

Types of Drama
- Comedy
- Tragedy
- Drama

Comparing Literary Works:
Characters

developed through

motives

traits

(demonstrated in these selections)

Selection names:
1.
2.

Student Log

Complete this chart to track your assignments.

Writing	Extend Your Learning	Writing Workshop	Other Assignments

5

from **Dragonwings** by Laurence Yep
Vocabulary Warm-up Word Lists

Study these words from Dragonwings. Then, apply your knowledge to the activities that follow.

Word List A

audience [AW dee uhns] *n.* group of watchers or listeners
The <u>audience</u> applauded wildly after the exciting performance.

contraption [kuhn TRAP shuhn] *n.* odd device or gadget
The strange <u>contraption</u> had weird levers and buttons, so we didn't know how to start it.

demonstration [dem uhn STRAY shuhn] *n.* outward showing
In <u>demonstration</u> of her anger, Cassie stamped her foot.

flight [FLYT] *adj.* relating to the act or manner of flying
Hector wanted to be a pilot, so he enrolled in <u>flight</u> school.

haul [HAWL] *v.* pull with force; drag
Bruce and Cara <u>haul</u> their equipment from the car to the campsite.

repeat [ree PEET] *v.* to do over again
Samantha will <u>repeat</u> her talent-show performance on Friday.

serious [SEER ee uhs] *adj.* giving cause for concern; dangerous
After a <u>serious</u> car accident, Bryan was taken to the hospital.

steep [STEEP] *adj.* having a sharp slope or incline
The mountain we climbed is very <u>steep</u> and high.

Word List B

expected [ek SPEKT ed] *v.* looked for as likely to happen
Casey <u>expected</u> a raise in her allowance when she turned twelve.

immigration [im i GRAY shun] *adj.* coming into a foreign country to live there
Mr. Moreno checked Lupe's <u>immigration</u> status before hiring her.

laundry [LAWN dree] *n.* commercial establishment for washing and ironing clothing
The <u>laundry</u> is a profitable family business for the Johnsons.

machines [muh SHEENZ] *n.* mechanical devices or equipment
Sixteen sewing <u>machines</u> were set up in four rows in the factory.

merchants [MER chuhnts] *n.* persons who buy and sell things for profit; storekeepers
Stu and Don had been <u>merchants</u> at the same location for ten years.

probably [PRAHB uh blee] *adv.* likely; presumably
The weather is good, so the plane will <u>probably</u> land on time.

recover [ree KUHV uhr] *v.* to get well
It took Steven ten days to <u>recover</u> from the flu.

separated [SEP uh rayt ed] *v.* came apart
The glue was weak, so the decorations <u>separated</u> from the frame.

Name _____ Date _____

from *Dragonwings* by Laurence Yep
Vocabulary Warm-up Exercises

Exercise A *Fill in each blank in the paragraph below with an appropriate word from Word List A. Use each word only once.*

Nobody could figure out how to use the strange [1] _____, so they had to ask Jack, the inventor, for a [2] _____. A group of assistants helped Jack [3] _____ the machine to the stage. The [4] _____ watched as Jack pressed a red button. Suddenly the propeller began turning. Jack, standing too close, got hit by the twisting blades. His assistants thought he was hurt, but it was not [5] _____. "Let me [6] _____ what I said earlier," said Jack. "This machine can push heavy loads up [7] _____ inclines. For example, a [8] _____ attendant could easily push a serving cart to the front of the plane, even if the plane were still ascending!"

Exercise B *Answer the questions with complete sentences or explanations.*

1. Why might egg yolks and egg whites be <u>separated</u>?
   _____

2. If you <u>expected</u> to win a special award, what preparations might you make?
   _____

3. Name two <u>machines</u> you might use at home.
   _____

4. What does an <u>immigration</u> officer do?
   _____

5. If you dropped your clothes off at a <u>laundry</u>, what would you want done with them?
   _____

6. What do <u>merchants</u> do to earn money?
   _____

7. If Alex says he will <u>probably</u> go to a party, will he be there for sure?
   _____

8. How long did it take you to <u>recover</u> the last time you got sick?
   _____

Name _____ Date _____

from **Dragonwings** by Laurence Yep
Reading Warm-up A

Read the following passage. Pay special attention to the underlined words. Then, read it again, and complete the activities. Use a separate sheet of paper for your written answers.

Imagine for a moment that you are with the Wright brothers near Kitty Hawk, North Carolina. The year is 1903. It is eight days before Christmas. You are excited to be among the small <u>audience</u> waiting to see if they will actually fly this time. Besides you and the Wrights, four men and a boy are there to witness this <u>demonstration</u>.

Yesterday, Wilbur had made an attempt, but the <u>contraption</u> they called an "aeroplane" had barely made it off the ground. Would today be any different? Yesterday, they had tried to fly from the top of a <u>steep</u> hill. Today, they would try to take off from flat ground instead. By aiming the plane into the wind, they figured they had a better chance to get aloft.

The men had helped the Wrights <u>haul</u> the plane to the sand bar at Kitty Hawk. It weighs about 600 pounds, and its two pairs of wings are about 40 feet across, so it had been quite a job to get it in place. Now, you watch as Orville climbs out on the lower wing. He stretches out face down. His legs hang out beyond the wing. Wilbur ties a strap around his brother's hips so he won't fall off. Wilbur starts the engine as Orville grips the controls. The plane moves forward, rising ten feet in the air. The boy who's watching this with you starts shouting. "He's flying! He's flying!" One of the men takes a photograph. The <u>flight</u> time is 12 seconds, as Orville flies 120 feet. The brothers take turns flying a few more times that day. The longest flight is done by Wilbur, who flies 852 feet in 59 seconds.

A strong wind finally tips the plane over. The damage is <u>serious</u>, and the plane needs major repairs. Soon, though, the Wrights plan to <u>repeat</u> the experiment, and you hope they'll invite you again.

1. Underline the sentence that tells how many people are in the small <u>audience</u>. What did you see the last time you were part of an *audience*?

2. Underline the words that tell what the audience will do at the <u>demonstration</u>. Use *demonstration* in a sentence.

3. Circle the word that tells what the Wrights called their <u>contraption</u>. Use *contraption* in a sentence.

4. Underline the word that means the opposite of <u>steep</u>. Would you rather climb a *steep* hill or walk on a flat beach? Explain.

5. Circle the words that tell where the men had to <u>haul</u> the plane. Describe the last time you had to *haul* something heavy from one place to another.

6. Underline the phrases that give information about the <u>flight</u> time, or how far they went and how fast. What does *flight* mean?

7. Circle the words that explain why the damage is considered <u>serious</u>. Write a sentence using the word *serious*.

8. Underline the words that tell what the Wrights plan to <u>repeat</u>. What does *repeat* mean?

Name _____ Date _____

from **Dragonwings** by Laurence Yep
Reading Warm-up B

Read the following passage. Pay special attention to the underlined words. Then, read it again, and complete the activities. Use a separate sheet of paper for your written answers.

After the Civil War, people from other countries began moving to the United States in great numbers. In part, this was due to the abolition of slavery. In need of a cheap labor pool to <u>recover</u> from the war, America welcomed the poor, who <u>expected</u> to work for very little pay. Most of these immigrants came from Germany, Ireland, and England. A smaller percentage of the immigrants came from China.

The Chinese had first been drawn to this country by the California gold rush that began in 1849. As they came through the <u>immigration</u> station in San Francisco, they were welcomed at first. This is <u>probably</u> because they worked hard and kept to themselves. They were also willing to accept low pay. Most of these immigrants were young male peasants. They had left their rural villages to labor in the American West. <u>Separated</u> from their families, they worked on the railroads. They also mined for gold and other minerals.

As these economic opportunities declined, the Chinese looked elsewhere for work. Some opened businesses that did <u>laundry</u> for people who didn't want to wash and iron their own clothes. Others took low-paying factory jobs, working at various <u>machines</u> to produce manufactured goods.

By the 1870s, hard times forced other groups to compete with the Chinese for humble jobs. Hostility toward the Chinese soon developed. In 1882, Congress passed the Chinese Exclusion Act; between 1882 and 1965, only <u>merchants</u> (such as shopkeepers and traders), diplomats, and students and their dependents were allowed to travel to the United States.

Laws passed in the 1960s restored many basic rights to Chinese Americans. Since the 1970s, two types of Chinese immigrants have been coming to the United States. The first group is wealthy and well-educated. The second group includes those who are fleeing poverty and other hardships.

1. Underline the words that tell from what America needed to <u>recover</u>. What might you do to try to *recover* from a disappointment?

2. Circle the words that tell what the poor immigrants <u>expected</u>. Write a sentence using the word *expected*.

3. Underline the words that tell what happened when the Chinese arrived at the <u>immigration</u> station. What does *immigration* mean?

4. Circle the words that explain why these immigrants were <u>probably</u> welcomed at first. Then, rewrite the sentence, replacing *probably* with words that have a similar meaning.

5. Underline the words that tell from whom the immigrants were <u>separated</u>. Use *separated* in a sentence.

6. Circle the words that describe customers for the <u>laundry.</u> What items might you find at a *laundry*?

7. Underline the words that tell what the <u>machines</u> did. What are *machines*?

8. Circle the words that further explain what <u>merchants</u> are. Use *merchants* in a sentence.

Laurence Yep
Listening and Viewing

Segment 1: Meet Laurence Yep
• Why did Laurence Yep identify with the themes he encountered in science fiction?
• Does it surprise you that he chose to write science fiction? Why or why not?

_____

_____

_____

Segment 2: Drama
• According to Yep, what are the differences between a drama and a novel?
• Which form, the drama or the novel, might be more difficult to write? Why?

_____

_____

_____

Segment 3: The Writing Process
• Why does Yep adjust his drafts as he writes?
• What method of Yep's would you be most inclined to try in your own writing? Why?

_____

_____

_____

Segment 4: The Rewards of Writing
• What does Yep think literature can do for young readers?

_____

_____

_____

Name _____   Date _____

Learning About Drama

Drama is a story told in dialogue by performers in front of an audience. The **playwright** is the author of a drama, which may also be called a *play*. The play itself is written in segments, called **acts.** Acts are often divided into **scenes.**

A playwright uses **characterization** to create believable characters. To advance the action, the playwright creates **dramatic speech.** Two types of dramatic speech are **dialogue,** conversation between two or more characters, and **monologue,** a long speech by a single character. A monologue often reveals a character's thoughts and feelings.

Stage directions describe the scenery and tell how the characters move and speak. The **set** is the construction onstage that suggests the time and place of the action (the setting). **Props** are small movable items that make the set look realistic.

Two types of drama are comedy and tragedy. A **comedy** has a happy ending. It often features ordinary characters in funny situations. In a **tragedy,** the events lead to the downfall of the main character. The main character may be an ordinary person, but the traditional tragic hero is a man of great significance, such as a king.

A. DIRECTIONS: *Read the following excerpt from a drama. Then, answer the questions.*

[*The FISCHERS' kitchen, 7 A.M. MRS. FISCHER sits at kitchen table, reading a newspaper. The door opens. BECKY rushes in. She wears school clothes and carries a book bag.*]

BECKY. Mom! I overslept! I'll miss the tryouts for the play. Why didn't you wake me?

MRS. FISCHER [*getting up from the table*]. Calm down. Let me make you some breakfast.

BECKY [*almost shouting*]. Breakfast? I'm already late!

MRS. FISCHER [*patiently*]. No, dear, you're early. It's Saturday. Tryouts aren't until Monday.

1. Describe the set. _____

2. What props are used? _____

3. Quote a stage direction that tells how a character speaks.

   _____

4. Quote a stage direction that tells how a character moves.

   _____

5. Is the passage a dialogue or a monologue? Explain.

   _____

6. Is this scene more likely from a comedy or a tragedy? Explain. _____

   _____

Name _____ Date _____

from **Dragonwings** by Laurence Yep
Model Selection: Drama

Dragonwings is a **drama,** or *play*, a story told in dialogue and meant to be performed by actors before an audience. Laurence Yep is the **playwright,** the author of the play. A play is written in segments. You have read just one segment, a **scene.** In a full-length work, several scenes usually make up an **act,** and several acts make up the play.

To advance the action, Yep wrote **dramatic speech.** Most of the excerpt from *Dragonwings* contains **dialogue,** conversation between several characters. One section might be considered a **monologue,** a long speech by a single character. A monologue often reveals a character's thoughts and feelings.

Stage directions describe the scenery and sound effects and tell how the characters move and speak. The **set** is the construction onstage that suggests the time and place of the action (the setting). **Props** are small movable items that make the set look realistic.

In a drama, as the **main character** develops, the audience should identify with his or her emotions. The **climax** of a drama, the moment of greatest tension, concerns the main character in some way. With the climax comes some insight or revelation.

A. DIRECTIONS: *Answer these questions about Scene 9 of* Dragonwings.

1. What is the setting? _____

2. What props is Moon Shadow most likely using during his opening speech?

   _____

3. Describe one sound effect that is used. _____

4. After Windrider takes off in the airplane, Moon Shadow speaks these lines:

   I thought he'd fly forever and ever. Up, up to heaven and never come down. But then . . . Dragonwings came crashing to earth. Father had a few broken bones, but it was nothing serious. Only the aeroplane was wrecked. . . . Father didn't say much, just thought a lot I figured he was busy designing the next aeroplane. . . .

   What type of dramatic speech would you call this passage? Explain your answer.

   _____

5. Who is the main character? How can you tell?

   _____

   _____

B. DIRECTIONS: *What is the climax of events in Scene 9 of* Dragonwings? *What insight does Windrider gain in response to the climax? What insight does Moon Shadow gain?*

_____

_____

_____

Name _____   Date _____

from **Dragonwings** by Laurence Yep
Open-Book Test

Short Answer *Write your responses to the questions in this section on the lines provided.*

1. You are reading a long speech that is spoken by a single character. As the character speaks, he or she reveals private thoughts and feelings. Are you reading a monologue or a dialogue? Explain.

   _____

   _____

   _____

2. Playwrights provide stage directions to help directors and actors perform a play. What three types of information can be found in stage directions?

   _____

   _____

   _____

3. In a scene in a play, an actor might use a key to unlock a door. What dramatic element is the key? Why might the actor use a real key?

   _____

   _____

4. In the chart below, explain the elements of a screenplay, a teleplay, and a radio play. Then, answer the questions that follow the chart.

Screenplay	Teleplay	Radio Play

   What is your favorite novel?_____

   Would your favorite novel make a good screenplay, teleplay, or radio play? Why or why not?

   _____

   _____

   _____

   _____

   _____

5. The first line of Scene 9 of Laurence Yep's *Dragonwings* is *Piedmont, later that day outside the stable.* What does this tell the reader? What element of drama is it?

_____

_____

6. Uncle Bright Star starts a chant at the bottom of the hill in Scene 9 of *Dragonwings.* What is the purpose of his chant?

_____

_____

7. What does the playwright want the audience to hear at the top of the hill in the middle of Scene 9 of *Dragonwings?* What dramatic element communicates this information?

_____

_____

_____

8. Toward the end of Scene 9 of *Dragonwings*, Windrider is turning, free as an eagle. What name does the stage direction give to these movements? What does this movement represent?

_____

_____

_____

9. At the end of Scene 9 of *Dragonwings*, what does Windrider suggest will likely happen? Explain.

_____

_____

_____

10. Who is the main character of *Dragonwings*? How do you know?

_____

_____

Essay

Write an extended response to the question of your choice or to the question or questions your teacher assigns you.

11. Toward the end of Scene 9 of *Dragonwings,* Windrider tells Moon Shadow that he has decided to give up flying to go work in a laundry and bring his wife from China. In an essay, tell what those decisions reveal about Windrider. What kind of man is he? How has he changed? Mention details from the scene to support your ideas.

12. At the end of Scene 9 of *Dragonwings*, Windrider hands his cap to Moon Shadow. In an essay, explain why Laurence Yep includes this stage direction in his play. Why does the stage direction say that Moon Shadow puts the cap on at the end of the scene, when he appears as an adult?

13. At the end of Scene 9 of *Dragonwings*, Moon Shadow says that they never flew again, and adds, "But dreams stay with you, and we never forgot." In an essay, explain what these last lines tell you. Why is it important that father and son never forgot their experience? How do you think it might have affected their later lives? Use details from the play to support your answer.

14. **Thinking About the Big Question: Do others see us more clearly than we see ourselves?** At the end of *Dragonwings,* Windrider describes seeing Moon Shadow from the air. Respond to these questions in an essay: Does Windrider really see his son? How does seeing his son from the air change him?

Oral Response

15. Go back to question 4, 8, or 10 or to the question your teacher assigns you. Take a few minutes to expand your answer and prepare an oral response. Find additional details in *Dragonwings* that support your points. If necessary, make notes to guide your oral response.

Name _____ Date _____

from Dragonwings by Laurence Yep
Selection Test A

Learning About Drama *Identify the letter of the choice that best answers the question.*

____ 1. Which of the following is the best definition of drama?
   A. a story with props
   B. a story with a happy ending
   C. a story told in dialogue by performers
   D. a story in which the main character eventually fails

____ 2. Which statement correctly describes a monologue?
   A. A monologue is a serious speech spoken only in a tragedy.
   B. A monologue is a short speech spoken by one character.
   C. A monologue is a long speech spoken by one character.
   D. A monologue is a conversation between several characters.

____ 3. Which term describes the constructions that suggest the time and place of the action of a play?
   A. stage
   B. set
   C. act
   D. scene

____ 4. Which of the following is an example of a prop?
   A. a door at the back of the stage
   B. a pair of crutches that a character uses
   C. a direction telling how a character moves
   D. a long speech in the opening scene

____ 5. Which line contains a stage direction that tells how the actor playing John should speak?
   A. JOHN [*throwing his book*]. I don't understand the problem.
   B. JOHN. What time does the physics test begin?
   C. JOHN [*shaking his head*]. I'll never be a rocket scientist.
   D. JOHN [*pleading*]. You've got to help me.

____ 6. Which statement is true of every comedy?
   A. It has a happy ending.
   B. It contains sound effects.
   C. It contains unusal animals.
   D. It features at least one clown.

Name _____ Date _____

Critical Reading

___ 7. The first line of Scene 9 of *Dragonwings* is
> Piedmont, later that day, outside the stable.

What does this line tell the reader?
A. which characters are onstage
B. where and when the scene takes place
C. how the characters are to act
D. whether this is a comedy or a tragedy

___ 8. At the beginning of Scene 9 of *Dragonwings*, Moon Shadow is writing a letter. To whom is he writing?
A. Miss Whitlaw
B. Black Dog
C. his uncle
D. his mother

___ 9. What is the relationship between Moon Shadow and Windrider in *Dragonwings*?
A. Windrider is Moon Shadow's brother.
B. Windrider is Moon Shadow's uncle.
C. Windrider is Moon Shadow's father.
D. Windrider is Moon Shadow's teacher.

___ 10. Which statement is true about Uncle Bright Star in *Dragonwings*?
A. He has come to help although he does not think the plane will fly.
B. He refuses to help because he thinks planes are unreliable.
C. He is worried that Moon Shadow will not speak to him again.
D. He is angry because Windrider has refused to return to China.

___ 11. In Scene 9 of *Dragonwings*, what action do the characters perform without props, in a pantomime?
A. taking the harness off Uncle's horse
B. dragging the plane to the top of the hill
C. pulling down on the propellers of the plane
D. reading a newspaper article about the flight

___ 12. What does Uncle Bright Star do in Scene 9 of *Dragonwings* to help the characters work together?
A. He turns the propeller.
B. He drives the wagon.
C. He dances a ballet.
D. He leads a chant.

_____ 13. What is the purpose of Windrider's ballet in Scene 9 of *Dragonwings*?
   A. to show how creative he is
   B. to emphasize his love for Moon Shadow
   C. to express his hopes for the future
   D. to represent the flight of the airplane

_____ 14. What do the sound effects in Scene 9 of *Dragonwings* allow the audience to hear?
   A. the movement of the horse
   B. the cheering of the crowds
   C. the flight of the plane
   D. the crash of the plane

_____ 15. After the plane takes off in Scene 9 of *Dragonwings*, what happens to it?
   A. It grows smaller and then disappears.
   B. Windrider sells it to start a laundry.
   C. It crashes to the ground and breaks apart.
   D. It glides to the ground but is not damaged.

Essay

16. Toward the end of Scene 9 of *Dragonwings*, Windrider tells Moon Shadow that he has decided to give up flying to go to work in a laundry and bring his wife from China. In an essay, tell what those decisions say about Windrider. What kind of man is he? How has he changed? Mention two details from the scene to support your ideas.

17. At the end of Scene 9 of *Dragonwings*, Moon Shadow says that he and his father talked about flying, but they never actually flew again. Moon Shadow says,

> But dreams stay with you, and we never forgot.

In an essay, tell what you think Moon Shadow means by these lines.

18. **Thinking About the Big Question: Do others see us more clearly than we see ourselves?** At the end of *Dragonwings*, Windrider describes seeing Moon Shadow from the air. Does Windrider really see his son? How does seeing his son from the air change him? Explain your answers in an essay supported by examples from the selection.

Name _____ Date _____

Selection Test B

Learning About Drama *Identify the letter of the choice that best completes the statement or answers the question.*

_____ 1. A book that a character reads in a scene from a play is an example of
    A. a stage direction.   C. a prop.
    B. a set.   D. a monologue.

_____ 2. Which of the following is the best definition of dialogue?
    A. a conversation between characters in a play
    B. the conflict that the characters in a play face
    C. the downfall of the main character in a play
    D. a long speech by a character in a play

_____ 3. Stage directions may indicate
    I. the tone of voice an actor should use
    II. an action an actor should take
    III. the scenery
    IV. sound effects
    A. I and II
    B. I, II, and IV
    C. III and IV
    D. I, II, III, and IV

_____ 4. Which statement is true of every tragedy?
    A. The events lead to a happy ending.
    B. The main character is someone of significance.
    C. The events lead to the downfall of the main character.
    D. The main character reveals his or her inner thoughts at the climax.

_____ 5. Which statement is true of a screenplay?
    A. It is better suited to comedy than to tragedy.
    B. It contains dialogue but never includes a monologue.
    C. The stage directions do not refer to the setting.
    D. The stage directions may refer to camera angles.

_____ 6. Which statement is true of every comedy?
    A. The main character is very funny.
    B. Clowns appear in one or more scenes.
    C. The ending is a happy one.
    D. The characters are unrealistic.

Critical Reading

_____ 7. Scene 9 of *Dragonwings* is set
    A. outside a stable.
    B. in a stable.
    C. in a laundry near San Francisco.
    D. at Uncle Bright Star's home in Piedmont.

____ 8. What event takes place as Scene 9 of *Dragonwings* opens?
   A. Uncle Bright Star stamps his feet to get everyone moving.
   B. Miss Whitlaw knocks on the door of the stable.
   C. Moon Shadow writes a letter to his mother.
   D. Windrider climbs into his airplane.

____ 9. At the beginning of Scene 9 of *Dragonwings*, the audience learns that Moon Shadow
   A. owes Miss Whitlaw a lot of money.
   B. has had everything stolen by Black Dog.
   C. is about to move back to China.
   D. does not believe airplanes can fly.

____ 10. In Scene 9 of *Dragonwings*, why is Moon Shadow surprised that Uncle Bright Star has come to help?
   A. Uncle Bright Star is old and in poor health.
   B. Uncle Bright Star has stolen from Windrider.
   C. Uncle Bright Star has traveled a great distance.
   D. Uncle Bright Star does not believe the plane will fly.

____ 11. In Scene 9 of *Dragonwings*, Windrider and the others go through the motions of pulling on ropes without actually using ropes. In doing so, they are
   A. using sound effects.
   B. using props.
   C. pantomiming.
   D. dancing.

____ 12. In Scene 9 of *Dragonwings*, the characters must drag the plane to the top of the hill because
   A. the wheels on the plane have gotten hopelessly stuck in the mud.
   B. the winds at the top of the hill are blowing in the right direction.
   C. Red Rabbit is too tired to pull everyone up the hill in the wagon.
   D. Miss Whitlaw has asked them to take the plane off her property.

____ 13. Uncle Bright Star starts a chant in Scene 9 of *Dragonwings* because
   A. he believes that if he prays, the plane will fly.
   B. he wants to impress Miss Whitlaw with his knowledge.
   C. he believes a chant will give Windrider confidence.
   D. he wants everyone to work at the same pace.

____ 14. In Scene 9 of *Dragonwings*, Windrider does a ballet in order to
   A. represent the act of flying a plane.
   B. thank Uncle Bright Star for helping.
   C. provide Miss Whitlaw with entertainment.
   D. demonstrate an aspect of his culture.

____ 15. What event occurs at the climax of Scene 9 of *Dragonwings*?
A. Uncle Bright Star joins Windrider in the airplane.
B. Dragonwings starts to fall but then levels off.
C. Windrider succeeds in making the plane fly.
D. Moon Shadow's mother reveals her secret.

____ 16. At the end of Scene 9 of *Dragonwings*, Moon Shadow
A. gives his cap to his father.
B. appears onstage as an adult.
C. decides that he will someday fly a plane.
D. decides to return to China to visit his mother.

____ 17. According to Scene 9 of *Dragonwings*, the flight of Dragonwings is not a complete success because
A. the plane crashes and breaks apart.
B. Windrider flies off and never returns.
C. Windrider vows never to fly again.
D. Miss Whitlaw is disappointed.

____ 18. At the end of Scene 9 of *Dragonwings*, Uncle Bright Star offers
A. to bring Windrider's wife from China.
B. to help Windrider build a new airplane.
C. Windrider the money to return to China.
D. Windrider a partnership in his laundry.

____ 19. Who is the main character of *Dragonwings*?
A. Windrider
B. Uncle Bright Star
C. Miss Whitlaw
D. Moon Shadow

Essay

20. At the end of Scene 9 of *Dragonwings*, Windrider hands his cap to Moon Shadow. In an essay, explain what this action might symbolize. Why does Moon Shadow wear the cap at the end of the scene, when he appears as an adult?

21. At the end of Scene 9 of *Dragonwings*, Moon Shadow appears as an adult and puts on Windrider's cap. He says,

> We always talked about flying again. Only we never did. . . . But dreams stay with you, and we never forgot.

In an essay, explain what these last lines tell you. How would the scene have been different if it had ended just before, with Windrider speaking the final lines?

22. **Thinking About the Big Question: Do others see us more clearly than we see ourselves?** At the end of *Dragonwings*, Windrider describes seeing Moon Shadow from the air. Respond to these questions in an essay: Does Windrider really see his son? How does seeing his son from the air change him?

Vocabulary Warm-up Word Lists

Study these words from A Christmas Carol: Scrooge and Marley, *Act I. Then, complete the activities that follow.*

Word List A

gold [GOHLD] *n.* yellowish precious metal
   The gold used to make the necklace was of high quality.

lustrous [LUHS truhs] *adj.* shining or bright
   In the sunlight, Donna's hair looked shiny and lustrous.

miser [MY zuhr] *n.* stingy person who hoards his or her wealth
   Jay was a miser when it came to sharing his dessert with others.

penance [PEN uhns] *n.* voluntary act to show that one is sorry for a misdeed
   Ann decided that her penance for losing her temper with Molly was taking Molly to dinner.

perfection [puhr FEK shuhn] *n.* condition of being perfect or excellent
   The beautiful colors of the sunset were a vision of perfection.

replenish [ri PLEN ish] *v.* to make full or complete again by supplying a new stock
   Dot will replenish our supply of juice when she goes to the store.

resolute [REZ uh loot] *adj.* determined, unwavering
   With a resolute look, Alex set out to hike the entire length of the trail.

shrivels [SHRIV uhlz] *v.* wrinkles or becomes withered or shrunken
   The last rose of summer shrivels after it has bloomed.

Word List B

bleak [BLEEK] *adj.* cold, harsh, or dreary
   The constant rain gave us very damp, bleak weather.

dismal [DIZ muhl] *adj.* gloomy, miserable
   The dismal expression on Dave's face told us the race had not gone well.

establishments [i STAB lish muhntz] *n.* businesses; public or private structures
   The popular restaurant chain had many establishments.

grindstone [GRYND stohn] *n.* flat millstone for grinding grain into flour
   Dan always has his nose to the grindstone, working hard all the time.

impropriety [im pruh PRY i tee] *n.* improper action or behavior
   Margo's impropriety was that she never wrote thank-you notes.

neglected [ni GLEKT ed] *adj.* not properly cared for; ignored
   The neglected kitten badly needed warmth and food.

surviving [suhr VYV ing] *adj.* remaining alive; still living or existing
   The surviving spouse will continue to live in the house.

welfare [WEL fayr] *n.* well-being
   Bella was concerned about the welfare of her pet hamster.

A Christmas Carol: Scrooge and Marley, *Act I* by Israel Horovitz
Vocabulary Warm-up Exercises

Exercise A *Fill in each blank in the paragraph below with an appropriate word from Word List A. Use each word only once.*

Cindy liked to grow flowers, and her favorites were sunflowers that shone as bright as [1] _____. To her, there was nothing else as pretty—they were [2] _____! One day, Cindy's friend Michelle asked her if she could have a sunflower for a bouquet. Cindy said no, and Michelle called her a greedy [3] _____. "I hope each of your flowers dries up and [4] _____!" said Michelle. Cindy immediately was sorry she had not shared the flower with her friend. For her [5] _____ she put several sunflowers in a [6] _____ copper vase. Marching to Michelle's house in a [7] _____ way, Cindy apologized and gave the flowers to her friend. Michelle smiled and offered to help Cindy plant more flowers to [8] _____ her supply.

Exercise B *Find a **synonym** for each word in the following vocabulary list. Use each synonym in a sentence that makes the meaning of the word clear.*

Example: Vocabulary word: dismal   Synonym: *gloomy*
    Sample sentence: The <u>gloomy</u> dimness of the room was depressing.

1. establishments _____
_____

2. welfare _____
_____

3. impropriety _____
_____

4. bleak _____
_____

5. grindstone _____
_____

6. surviving _____
_____

7. neglected _____
_____

Name _____ Date _____

A Christmas Carol: Scrooge and Marley, *Act I* by Israel Horovitz
Reading Warm-up A

Read the following passage. Pay special attention to the underlined words. Then, read it again, and complete the activities. Use a separate sheet of paper for your written answers.

This is the legend of King Midas, a greedy <u>miser</u> who hoarded all his valuables. It is said that more than anything, Midas loved shiny, yellow <u>gold</u>. This story tells how his love of it almost destroyed him.

Here is what happened. One day, King Midas met an important follower of the Greek god Dionysus. Midas let the man stay with him for a while, and then he guided the man back to Dionysus. Grateful for what he had done for his follower, the god told Midas he would grant him one wish.

At once, Midas requested that anything he touch be turned to gold. That ability would allow him to always <u>replenish</u> his supply of gold and to amass as large a fortune as he wanted. Dionysus granted the king's wish.

Midas immediately wanted to try it out, so on his way home he broke off a tree branch. It immediately turned to gold. "What <u>perfection</u>!" exclaimed Midas, admiring the brilliant, <u>lustrous</u> metal. He rejoiced, for now he would be the richest man on earth.

His happiness was not to last, however. For when he told his servants to bring a feast of celebration to him, he lifted a cup to drink. The cup and the liquid in it turned to gold. Next, he took a piece of bread. It, too, turned to gold. He suddenly realized that without food and drink, he could not live, just as a plant without sunlight <u>shrivels</u> and dies.

He began to realize that all his riches could not help him solve this dilemma. With a determined and <u>resolute</u> spirit, he prayed for Dionysus to undo the wish. He promised he would do whatever <u>penance</u> he could to make up for his greed. The god took pity on the king and told him how to undo the spell. From that day on, King Midas detested riches. He lived the rest of his life simply, enjoying what nature had to offer.

1. Circle the words that tell why Midas was a greedy <u>miser</u>. Use *miser* in a sentence.

2. Underline the words that describe how <u>gold</u> looks. What things might be made of *gold*?

3. Circle the words that tell what Midas wanted to <u>replenish</u>. Define *replenish*.

4. Underline the words that tell what was <u>perfection</u> to King Midas. What is *perfection* to you?

5. Circle the synonym for <u>lustrous</u>. Use *lustrous* in a sentence.

6. Underline the words that compare what happens to a plant that <u>shrivels</u> with what would happen to Midas. What does *shrivels* mean?

7. Underline the word that describes Midas's <u>resolute</u> spirit. Define *resolute*.

8. Circle the words that tell for what Midas promised to do <u>penance</u>. Why did he make that promise?

A Christmas Carol: Scrooge and Marley, *Act I* by Israel Horovitz
Reading Warm-up B

Read the following passage. Pay special attention to the underlined words. Then, read it again, and complete the activities. Use a separate sheet of paper for your written answers.

The Victorian Age in Britain was named after Queen Victoria. This era took place from the mid- to late 1800s. At that time, a great many children were not treated well. Poor children faced a bleak, hopeless future. They were sent to factories and other jobs to work long hours. Children whose families could afford to educate them might be sent away to boarding schools. Many of these establishments were run by strict and cruel headmasters, who regularly beat the students.

If a family was poor, or if one or both parents had died and the children were the surviving members of the family, the children were sent to work. Children earned less than adults, and their small hands were very nimble. These were two of the reasons that the owners of factories liked to hire children. Very little was done to safeguard the children's working conditions or welfare in these sweatshops. Children were often mangled by machinery. The shops were dismal, dirty places to work. The children toiled for long hours. They were powerless to rebel against these terrible conditions.

As a result of working long hours, always with their noses to the grindstone, the children and their families spent very little time together. Some children became servants in more wealthy households. The young servants had to follow many rules. It was an awful impropriety if they were seen or heard around the family for whom they worked.

Another common job for children was to become a chimney sweep. Again, their small size made them desirable for getting inside the chimneys to clean them. Burns, suffocation, and falls were common problems. Children were also used in the mines, where conditions were even worse, and many young workers perished.

The government and citizens of Victorian England badly neglected the basic needs of many children at work, school, and home.

1. Underline the word that is a synonym for bleak. What are some things you think are *bleak*?

2. Circle the words that tell what the establishments in the story are. Use *establishments* in a sentence.

3. Circle the words that tell more about what being surviving members of the family means. Define *surviving*.

4. Underline the words that give an example of how the welfare of the children was not safeguarded. What is *welfare*?

5. Underline the words that explain why the shops were dismal. Use *dismal* in a sentence.

6. Circle the words that tell why the children had their noses to the grindstone. Explain what this means.

7. Underline the words that tell what was an impropriety. Define *impropriety*.

8. Circle the words that tell what was neglected by people of Victorian England. What does *neglected* mean?

Name _____ Date _____

"A Christmas Carol: Scrooge and Marley, *Act 1*" by Israel Horowitz
Writing About the Big Question

Do others see us more clearly than we see ourselves?

Big Question Vocabulary

appearance	appreciate	assumption	bias	characteristic
define	focus	identify	ignore	image
perception	perspective	reaction	reflect	reveal

A. *Choose one word from the list above to complete each sentence. There may be more than one right answer.*

1. Over time, Betsy learned to _____ her mother's fashion advice.

2. Sometimes you know what a word means, but find it hard to _____.

3. Eric's hard work in the gym helped quicken his _____ time.

B. *Follow the directions in responding to each of the items below.*

1. List two different times when you learned something new about yourself. Write your response in complete sentences.

   _____

   _____

2. Choose one of the experiences you listed in number 1. Write three or more sentences describing that experience. Use at least two of the Big Question vocabulary words. You may use the words in different forms (for example you can change *reflect* to *reflection*).

   _____

   _____

C. *Complete the sentence below. Use the completed sentence as the topic sentence in a short paragraph about the big question.*

The way we treat others reveals _____

   _____

   _____

A Christmas Carol: Scrooge and Marley, *Act I,* by Israel Horovitz
Reading: Preview a Text to Set a Purpose for Reading

When you **set a purpose for reading,** you decide what you want to get from a text. Setting a purpose gives you a focus as you read. These are some of the reasons you might have for reading something:

- to learn about a subject
- to be entertained
- to gain understanding
- to prepare to take action or make a decision
- to find inspiration
- to complete a task

In order to set a purpose, **preview a text** before you read it. Look at the title, the pictures, the captions, the organization, and the beginnings of passages. If you already have a purpose in mind, previewing will help you decide whether the text will fit that purpose. If you do not have a purpose in mind, previewing the text will help you determine one.

DIRECTIONS: *Read the passages from Act I of* A Christmas Carol: Scrooge and Marley *indicated below, and then complete each item.*

1. Following the list of "The People of the Play," read the information labeled "The Place of the Play." Where is the play set?

   _____

2. Read the information labeled "The Time of the Play." When does the play take place?

   _____

3. What purpose or purposes might you set based on that information?

   _____

   _____

4. The illustrations that accompany the text of Act I of the play are photographs from a production of the play. Look at those photographs now, but ignore the one of the ghostly character in chains. How are the characters dressed?

   _____

5. Based on that information, what purpose might you set for reading Act I of the play?

   _____

6. Read the opening lines of Act I, Scene 1, spoken by a character called Marley. Then, look at the photograph of the ghostly character in chains. What purpose might you set based on that information?

   _____

A Christmas Carol: Scrooge and Marley, *Act I,* by Israel Horovitz
Literary Analysis: Dialogue

Dialogue is a conversation between characters. In a play, the characters are developed almost entirely through dialogue. Dialogue also advances the action of the plot and develops the conflict.

In the script of a dramatic work, you can tell which character is speaking by the name that appears before the character's lines. In this example of dialogue, you are introduced to two of the characters in *A Christmas Carol: Scrooge and Marley:*

NEPHEW. [*Cheerfully; surprising* SCROOGE] A merry Christmas to you, Uncle! God save you!

SCROOGE. Bah! Humbug!

NEPHEW. Christmas a "humbug," Uncle? I'm sure you don't mean that.

SCROOGE. I do! Merry Christmas? What right do you have to be merry? What reason have you to be merry? You're poor enough!

In just a few words apiece, the characters establish a conflict between them. The nephew thinks Christmas is a joyful holiday, and Scrooge thinks it is nonsense. This conflict will reappear throughout the play until it is resolved. Those lines of dialogue also give you a look at the character traits of Scrooge and his nephew. Scrooge is quarrelsome and unpleasant; the nephew is upbeat and friendly.

DIRECTIONS: *Answer the following questions about this passage from* A Christmas Carol: Scrooge and Marley, *Act I, Scene 2.*

PORTLY MAN. . . . [*Pen in hand; as well as notepad*] What shall I put you down for, sir?

SCROOGE. Nothing!

PORTLY MAN. You wish to be left anonymous?

SCROOGE. I wish to be left alone! [*Pauses; turns away; turns back to them*] Since you ask me what I wish, gentlemen, that is my answer. I help to support the establishments that I have mentioned; they cost enough: and those who are badly off must go there.

THIN MAN. Many can't go there; and many would rather die.

SCROOGE. If they would rather die, they had better do it, and decrease the surplus population. . . .

1. How many characters are speaking? Who are they?

   _____

2. What is Scrooge like in this scene?

   _____

3. How is he different from the men he is talking to?

   _____

   _____

4. Based on the identification of the characters, whom would you expect to speak next?

   _____

A Christmas Carol: Scrooge and Marley, *Act I,* by Israel Horovitz
Vocabulary Builder

Word List

conveyed   destitute   gratitude   implored   morose   void

A. DIRECTIONS: *Think about the meaning of the italicized word from the Word List in each sentence. Then, answer the question, and explain your answer.*

1. Marley *implored* Scrooge to pay attention to him. Did Marley ask casually?

   _____

2. Scrooge was *morose*. Did he enjoy celebrating Christmas?

   _____

3. Are the *destitute* able to save money?

   _____

4. Scrooge looked into the *void*. Did he see anything?

   _____

5. In Act I, Scene 3, of *A Christmas Carol: Scrooge and Marley*, has Scrooge *conveyed* his fear?

   _____

6. Do Fezziwig's employees feel *gratitude?*

   _____

B. WORD STUDY: *The Lation root -grat- means "thankful, pleasing." Read the following sentences. Use your knowledge of the root -grat- to write a full sentence to answer each question. Include the italicized word in your answer.*

1. If you are *grateful*, is it likely that someone has done something nice for you?

   _____

2. Is *gratitude* an unhappy emotion?

   _____

3. Would you value a *gratifying* friendship?

   _____

Name _____ Date _____

A Christmas Carol: Scrooge and Marley, *Act I,* by Israel Horovitz
Enrichment: Social Services

In Act I of *A Christmas Carol: Scrooge and Marley,* two men visit Scrooge's office to collect money for the needy. Scrooge refers to prisons, workhouses, the treadmill, and the Poor Law—all of which were used in nineteenth-century England to deal with people who were poverty-stricken. In the United States, more than 150 years after the events of *A Christmas Carol,* poverty is still a major problem. What do government and private agencies do today to try to help people in need?

A. DIRECTIONS: *Do research in a library, in a telephone directory, or on the Internet to find answers to the following questions.*

1. People whose earnings fall below the poverty line may be eligible to receive food stamps from the federal government. Where is the nearest office of the food-stamp agency in your area?

   _____

2. People in need may receive food, clothing, and shelter from organizations such as the Salvation Army. Where is the nearest Salvation Army center in your area? Where is the nearest soup kitchen? Is there another agency in your area that provides food, shelter, and clothing? If so, what is its name, and where is it located?

   _____

   _____

3. When people lose their home as a result of a fire, the American Red Cross often finds temporary shelter for them. Where is the nearest Red Cross office in your area?

   _____

4. Many senior citizens suffer from loneliness because they are unable to get around easily. Where is the nearest center providing services to senior citizens in your area?

   _____

5. Groups of people in communities often work together to help relieve the effects of poverty and hunger. Describe a group effort in your community. Who sponsors it? What is its mission?

   _____

B. DIRECTIONS: *Think about Ebenezer Scrooge's character in Act I of* A Christmas Carol: Scrooge and Marley *and his attitude toward people in need. Then, describe how you think Scrooge would react to one of the social services you learned about in doing your research for the first part of this activity. Would Scrooge be surprised by the service? Why or why not?*

   _____

   _____

Name _____ Date _____

A Christmas Carol: Scrooge and Marley, *Act I,* by Israel Horovitz
Integrated Language Skills: Grammar

Interjections

An **interjection** is a part of speech that exclaims and expresses a feeling, such as pain or excitement. It may stand on its own or it may appear within a sentence, but it functions independently of the sentence—it is not related to it grammatically. If an interjection stands on its own, it is set off with a period or an exclamation point. If it appears in a sentence, it is set off with commas.

> Wow, look at that sunset!
>
> My pants are covered with mud. Yuck!
>
> Boy, do my legs ache after climbing all those stairs.

Here are some common interjections:

Boy	Hmmm	Oh	Ugh	Whew	Yikes
Hey	Huh	Oops	Well	Wow	Yuck

A. DIRECTIONS: *Rewrite each item. Punctuate the sentence or pair of sentences to set off the interjections. Some sentences or pairs of sentences may be written in more than one way.*

1. Oops the cat spilled his food all over the floor

   _____

2. Ouch I dropped the hammer on my foot

   _____

3. I worked for two hours in the hot sun Whew

   _____

4. Hmmm I think this CD costs way too much

   _____

5. Hey do not go near that downed electric wire

   _____

B. WRITING APPLICATION: *Write three sentences using interjections. Be sure to punctuate the sentences correctly.*

1. _____

2. _____

3. _____

A Christmas Carol: Scrooge and Marley, *Act I,* by Israel Horovitz

Integrated Language Skills: Support for Writing a Letter

Use this form to prepare to **write a letter** to Scrooge.

Salutation

State your main point: Scrooge is missing out in life by being cranky and negative with the people around him.

State a specific thing that Scrooge is missing out on. Include a detail from the play or from your experience to support your point.

State another specific thing that Scrooge is missing out on. Include a detail from the play or from your experience to support your point.

Conclude with a summary or a request that Scrooge change his behavior.

Closing,

Signature

Dear _____,

_____
_____
_____
_____
_____
_____
_____
_____
_____
_____
_____
_____
_____
_____
_____
_____
_____
_____
_____
_____
_____
_____
_____
                          _____
                          _____

Now, prepare a final draft of your letter.

Name _____ Date _____

A Christmas Carol: Scrooge and Marley, *Act I,* by Israel Horovitz

Integrated Language Skills: Support for Extend Your Learning

Research and Technology

With the members of your group, consider the garments—the articles of clothing—that you must find out about in order to prepare **costume plans** for any two characters in *A Christmas Carol: Scrooge and Marley.* You will most likely want to consider these items:

men's pants   men's vest   men's tie   women's dress
men's shirt   men's jacket   men's hat   women's hat

You might each choose two or three garments to research. Remember that you are researching the clothing that people of Scrooge's class would have worn in England in the 1840s. Enter the information on this chart.

Garment	Description of Garment, Including Type of Fabric and Color

Unit 5 Resources: Drama
© Pearson Education, Inc. All rights reserved.
34

Name _____ Date _____

A Christmas Carol: Scrooge and Marley, *Act I*, by Israel Horovitz
Open-Book Test

Short Answer *Write your response to the questions in this section on the lines provided.*

1. The list of "The People of the Play" for Act I of *A Christmas Carol: Scrooge and Marley* includes characters with the names Portly Do-Gooder, The Ghost of Christmas Past, Fezziwig, and A Corpse. Explain which purpose you might set for reading after previewing these characters' names.

   _____

   _____

2. Jacob Marley speaks first in Act I, Scene 1, of *A Christmas Carol: Scrooge and Marley*. What does this speech tell you about Scrooge?

   _____

   _____

   _____

3. In the middle of Act I, Scene 2, of *A Christmas Carol: Scrooge and Marley*, Bob Cratchit speaks about Scrooge:

   CRATCHIT. Oh, mind him not, sir. He's getting on in years, and he's alone. He's noticed your visit. I'll wager your visit has warmed him.

   What does this dialogue tell you about Cratchit? Explain.

   _____

   _____

4. When Scrooge is at home in Act I, Scene 3, of *A Christmas Carol: Scrooge and Marley*, what does he do in the beginning of the scene that shows he is uneasy? Explain.

   _____

   _____

   _____

5. At first in Act I, Scene 3, of *A Christmas Carol: Scrooge and Marley*, Scrooge does not believe that the vision he sees is really Marley. How does he express his doubt?

   _____

   _____

6. According to Marley in the middle of Act I, Scene 3, of *A Christmas Carol: Scrooge and Marley*, why does he walk the earth as a spirit?

   _____

   _____

7. How does Fezziwig show benevolence in the middle of Act I, Scene 5, of *A Christmas Carol: Scrooge and Marley*? Base your answer on the meaning of *benevolence*.

   _____

   _____

8. When Scrooge and the young woman speak together toward the end of Act I, Scene 5, of *A Christmas Carol: Scrooge and Marley*, how does the plot advance? To answer the question, focus on what the audience learns.

   _____

   _____

   _____

9. The setting of Act I of *A Christmas Carol: Scrooge and Marley* is England, 1843. How does the dialogue help make the setting believable?

   _____

   _____

10. Three characters from Act I of *A Christmas Carol: Scrooge and Marley* remind Scrooge of important ideas from his past. Complete the chart with these ideas. Then, answer the question that follows.

Characters	**Importance to Scrooge**
Fan	
Fezziwig	
Woman	

   Which forgotten idea has the greatest impact on Scrooge? Why?_____

   _____

   _____

Essay

Write an extended response to the question of your choice or to the question or questions your teacher assigns you.

11. The conversation between Scrooge's nephew and Scrooge at the beginning of Act I, Scene 2, of *A Christmas Carol: Scrooge and Marley* shows each character's different ideas about Christmas. Respond to these questions in a brief essay: What is Scrooge's idea of Christmas? What does this tell you about the character of

Scrooge? What is the nephew's idea of Christmas? What does this tell you about the character of the nephew?

12. In Act I, Scene 5, of *A Christmas Carol: Scrooge and Marley*, the audience learns about Scrooge's life when he was younger. After seeing the younger Scrooge, do you feel more sympathy or less sympathy for the older Scrooge? In an essay, tell how Scrooge's experiences with the Ghost of Christmas Past make you feel about the Scrooge you first met in Act I, Scene 2.

13. When Scrooge tells Marley that Marley was always "a good man of business," in Act I, Scene 3, of *A Christmas Carol: Scrooge and Marley*, Marley responds.

    MARLEY. BUSINESS!!! Mankind was my business. The common welfare was my business; charity, mercy, forbearance, benevolence, were, all, my business.

    In an essay, explain what you think Marley means by these words. Cite a detail about Marley from the play to support your opinion.

14. **Thinking About the Big Question: Do others see us more clearly than we see ourselves?** What evidence in Act I of *A Christmas Carol: Scrooge and Marley* suggests that Marley sees the real Scrooge clearly? In an essay, explain how Marley sees his old partner. Cite examples from the play that support your ideas.

Oral Response

15. Go back to question 3, 4, or 8 or to the question your teacher assigns you. Take a few minutes to expand your answer and prepare an oral response. Find additional details in Act I of *A Christmas Carol: Scrooge and Marley* that support your points. If necessary, make notes to guide your oral response.

A Christmas Carol: Scrooge and Marley, *Act I*, by Israel Horovitz
Selection Test A

Critical Reading *Identify the letter of the choice that best answers the question.*

_____ 1. In Act I, Scene 1, of *A Christmas Carol: Scrooge and Marley*, what purpose might you set after reading this passage, spoken by Marley?

> [*Cackle-voiced*] My name is Jacob Marley and I am dead. . . . Oh, no, there's no doubt that I am dead. The register of my burial was signed by the clergyman, the clerk, the undertaker . . . and by my chief mourner . . . Ebenezer Scrooge. . . . I am dead as a doornail.

   A. to complete a task
   B. to take action or make a decision
   C. to gain understanding of a character
   D. to be inspired

_____ 2. Suppose your purpose for reading *A Christmas Carol: Scrooge and Marley* was to understand how people spoke in England in the mid-1800s. Which part of the play would be most helpful?
   A. the stage directions
   B. the cast of characters
   C. the dialogue
   D. the captions

_____ 3. Which purpose for reading might you set after previewing the photograph of Jacob Marley in Act I of *A Christmas Carol: Scrooge and Marley*?
   A. to learn about a subject
   B. to be entertained
   C. to take action
   D. to complete a task

_____ 4. What do you learn about Scrooge from Jacob Marley in Act I, Scene 1, of *A Christmas Carol: Scrooge and Marley*?
   A. He was a good friend to Marley.
   B. He often gives money to the poor.
   C. He is a solitary, miserly man.
   D. He likes cold, dark winter days.

___ 5. In Act I, Scene 2, of *A Christmas Carol: Scrooge and Marley*, what do you learn about the characters from the dialogue between Scrooge and his nephew?

A. They have different ideas about the worth of Christmas.

B. They have different ideas about the value of youth and age.

C. They have different ideas about how to run a business.

D. They have different ideas about the meaning of *humbug*.

___ 6. What do you learn about Bob Cratchit from his dialogue with Scrooge in Act I, Scene 2, of *A Christmas Carol: Scrooge and Marley*?

A. He fears Scrooge and plans to find a new job.

B. He understands Scrooge and pities him.

C. He is angry with Scrooge and plans to get revenge.

D. He is poor and hopes Scrooge will pay him more.

___ 7. In Act I, Scene 2, of *A Christmas Carol: Scrooge and Marley*, why does Scrooge object to people enjoying Christmas?

A. He is sad at Christmas because Marley died on Christmas Eve.

B. He actually likes Christmas and only pretends to dislike it.

C. He believes poor people should be unhappy even at Christmas.

D. He cares only for making money, and Christmas is an interruption.

___ 8. When Scrooge goes home in Act I, Scene 3, which actions show that he is uneasy?

I. He trims his candle as he walks.

II. He checks each of the rooms.

III. He looks under the sofa and table.

IV. He sees Marley's face in the pictures.

A. I, II, IV

B. II, III, IV

C. I, II, III

D. I, III, IV

___ 9. According to Act I, Scene 3, of *A Christmas Carol: Scrooge and Marley*, how did Marley get the chain that he wears?

A. It was given to him by the Ghost of Christmas Past.

B. It wrapped itself around him when he first screamed.

C. He created it to present to Scrooge as a gift.

D. He made it with his greed during his lifetime.

_____ **10.** What is revealed about Scrooge's childhood in Act I, Scene 5?

    A. He was alone and lonely.

    B. He was his father's favorite.

    C. He cared only about money.

    D. He was afraid of ghosts.

_____ **11.** According to the dialogue between the younger Scrooge and the woman in Act I, Scene 5, of *A Christmas Carol: Scrooge and Marley,* why is the woman ending their engagement?

    A. He is too interested in money.

    B. She thinks they are too young to marry.

    C. She believes he loves another woman.

    D. He calls her a mindless loon.

Vocabulary and Grammar

_____ **12.** In which of these lines is the meaning of the word *benevolence* best expressed?

    A. Many can't go there; and many would rather die.

    B. Oh, you'll be wanting the whole day tomorrow, I suppose?

    C. Whatever will it take to turn the faith of a miser from money to men?

    D. Father is so much kinder than he ever used to be.

_____ **13.** Which of these lines contains an interjection?

    A. And it's cheaper than painting in a new sign, isn't it?

    B. What else can I be? Eh?

    C. But you don't keep it, Uncle.

    D. Merry Christmas to you sir, and a very, very happy New Year.

Essay

14. The conversation between Scrooge's nephew and Scrooge in Act I, Scene 2, of *A Christmas Carol: Scrooge and Marley* shows each character's ideas about Christmas. In a brief essay, summarize those ideas.

15. What evidence in Act I of *A Christmas Carol: Scrooge and Marley* suggests that Marley is the best person, or character, to try to change Scrooge's life? In an essay, explain your ideas. Cite two details from the play to support your points.

16. **Thinking About the Big Question: Do others see us more clearly than we see ourselves?** In Act I of *A Christmas Carol: Scrooge and Marley,* we see contrasting views of Scrooge's personality. What evidence in this act suggests that Marley sees the real Scrooge clearly? In an essay, explain how Marley sees his old partner. Cite examples from the play that support your ideas.

A Christmas Carol: Scrooge and Marley, *Act I*, by Israel Horovitz
Selection Test B

Critical Reading *Identify the letter of the choice that best completes the statement or answers the question.*

____ 1. In Act I of *A Christmas Carol: Scrooge and Marley*, what purpose might you set for reading as you scan the list of "People in the Play" and see characters with such names as Portly Do-Gooder, The Ghost of Christmas Past, Fezziwig, and A Corpse?
   A. to complete a task
   B. to make a decision
   C. to gain understanding
   D. to be entertained

____ 2. In Act I of *A Christmas Carol: Scrooge and Marley*, what purpose might you set after reading this opening passage, spoken by Scrooge?

   They owe me money and I will collect. I will have them jailed, if I have to.

   A. to be inspired
   B. to gain understanding of a character
   C. to take action or make a decision
   D. to learn about a subject

____ 3. Suppose your purpose for reading Act I of *A Christmas Carol: Scrooge and Marley* is to be entertained. Which elements of the text would contribute to that purpose?
   A. the title
   B. the captions
   C. the photographs
   D. the stage directions

____ 4. What is the purpose of Marley's speech at the beginning of Act I, Scene 1, of *A Christmas Carol: Scrooge and Marley*?
   A. to present himself as the Ghost of Christmas Past
   B. to introduce the character of Scrooge to the audience
   C. to explain why he and Scrooge were once partners
   D. to tell Scrooge what to expect on Christmas Eve

____ 5. Which line of dialogue best describes Scrooge's nephew's ideas about Christmas?
   A. "Christmas a 'humbug,' Uncle? I'm sure you don't mean that."
   B. "[Christmas is] when men and women seem to open their shut-up hearts freely."
   C. "Don't be angry, Uncle. Come! Dine with us tomorrow."
   D. "I'll keep my Christmas humor to the last. So a Merry Christmas, Uncle!"

___ **6.** In Act I, what do you learn about Bob Cratchit from this dialogue?

> NEPHEW. [*To* CRATCHIT] He's impossible!
>
> CRATCHIT. Oh, mind him not, sir. He's getting on in years, and he's alone. He's noticed your visit. I'll wager your visit has warmed him.

A. He is angered by Scrooge.
B. He is forgiving of Scrooge.
C. He wishes he were Scrooge.
D. He agrees with Scrooge's nephew.

___ **7.** Which of these lines, spoken by Scrooge in Act I of *A Christmas Carol: Scrooge and Marley*, reveals that Scrooge has a sense of humor?
A. "It's not convenient, and it's not fair."
B. "There's more of gravy than of grave about you."
C. "But why do spirits such as you walk the earth?"
D. "I cannot in any way afford to lose my days."

___ **8.** In Act I, Scene 3, of *A Christmas Carol: Scrooge and Marley*, Scrooge does not believe that the vision he sees is in fact Marley. How does he express that doubt?
A. He says that he is seeing not Marley but a picture on the wall.
B. He says that someone is trying to frighten him or fool him.
C. He says that an undigested bit of food has affected his senses.
D. He says that someone who is dead could not appear before him.

___ **9.** According to Marley in Act I, Scene 3, why does he walk the earth as a spirit?
A. He was unsuccessful in his lifetime.
B. He committed crimes in his lifetime.
C. He never did anything in his lifetime except make money.
D. He cheated Scrooge in his lifetime and now must repay him.

___ **10.** In Act I, Scene 5, of *A Christmas Carol: Scrooge and Marley*, how does Scrooge respond to seeing the Christmas party of his former master, Fezziwig?
A. He thinks that he lavished too much praise on Fezziwig.
B. He realizes how much he has missed his sister, Fan.
C. He wishes he had given money to the boy singing carols.
D. He wishes he could say a word or two to Bob Cratchit.

___ **11.** In the dialogue between young Scrooge and the woman in Act I, Scene 5, of *A Christmas Carol: Scrooge and Marley*, what does the woman say has replaced her in Scrooge's life?
A. another woman
B. his desire for wealth
C. his wish to travel
D. a new career

___ 12. The dialogue between young Scrooge and the woman in Act I, Scene 5, of *A Christmas Carol: Scrooge and Marley* advances the plot by showing the audience
   A. that Scrooge was once romantic.
   B. how Scrooge grew to be so alone.
   C. that the woman Scrooge loved was poor.
   D. how easily Scrooge can win arguments.

Vocabulary and Grammar

___ 13. In which of these lines is the meaning of the word *implored* best expressed?
   A. "Mr. Marley has been dead these seven years."
   B. "Bah! Humbug! Christmas! Bah! Humbug!"
   C. "But you were always a good man of business, Jacob."
   D. "No, Jacob! Don't leave me! I'm frightened!"

___ 14. In which of these lines is the meaning of the word *destitute* suggested?
   A. "Many thousands are in want of common necessities."
   B. "Oh, you'll be wanting the whole day tomorrow, I suppose?"
   C. "This is a game in which I lose my senses!"
   D. "Fly, but I am a mortal and cannot fly!"

___ 15. Which of these lines does *not* contain an interjection?
   A. "Oh, Schoolmaster. I'd like you to meet my little sister."
   B. "Uh, well, goodbye, Schoolmaster. . . ."
   C. "Hilli-ho! Clear away, and let's have lots of room here!"
   D. "Even if I have grown so much wiser, what then?"

Essay

16. In Act I, Scene 5, of *A Christmas Carol: Scrooge and Marley*, when you learn what Scrooge was like when he was younger, do you feel more or less sympathy for him as an adult? In an essay, tell how Scrooge's experiences with the Ghost of Christmas Past make you feel about the Scrooge you see in Act I, Scene 2, of the play.

17. When Scrooge tells Marley that Marley was always "a good man of business," Marley responds:

   BUSINESS!!! Mankind was my business. The common welfare was my business; charity, mercy, forbearance, benevolence, were, all, my business.

In an essay, explain what you think Marley means by those words. Cite a detail about Marley that you have learned from the play to support your opinion.

18. **Thinking About the Big Question: Do others see us more clearly than we see ourselves?** What evidence in Act I of *A Christmas Carol: Scrooge and Marley* suggests that Marley sees the real Scrooge clearly? In an essay, explain how Marley sees his old partner. Cite examples from the play that support your ideas.

Vocabulary Warm-up Word Lists

Study these words from the play. Then, complete the activities.

Word List A

fortune [FAWR chuhn] *n.* wealth, riches
 The rich woman owned a <u>fortune</u> in real estate.

heartily [HAHRT uh lee] *adv.* sincerely and fully
 Joe welcomed his friend <u>heartily</u> with a warm handshake.

poem [POH uhm] *n.* a written piece that presents a powerful image or feeling, sometimes in rhyming, rhythmic words
 Jane read the <u>poem</u> about spring aloud to the class.

praise [PRAYZ] *v.* to express approval or admiration
 Did the students applaud and <u>praise</u> Bob's performance?

recollect [rek uh LEKT] *v.* to remember
 I can <u>recollect</u> each time I spent the summer at the beach.

thoughtful [THAWT fuhl] *adj.* meditative or full of thought
 After watching the serious play, Dawn became quiet and <u>thoughtful</u>.

unaltered [un AWL tuhrd] *adj.* unchanged
 Her positive attitude toward running track remained <u>unaltered</u> by the long practice hours.

value [VAL yoo] *n.* the worth of a thing
 What is the <u>value</u> of this old watch?

Word List B

beggars [BEG uhrz] *n.* people who beg or ask for charity
 Some of the homeless people were <u>beggars</u>.

consequence [KAHN si kwuhns] *n.* a result of an action
 The <u>consequence</u> of preparing for the test will likely be a good grade.

nasty [NAS tee] *adj.* very ill-humored or unpleasant
 The <u>nasty</u> dog snarled at the baby.

odious [OH dee uhs] *adj.* arousing or deserving of hatred or disgust
 Tina disliked the <u>odious</u> smell of the garbage.

preserved [pree ZERVD] *v.* saved or maintained
 We <u>preserved</u> Grandma's wedding dress by carefully wrapping it up.

refuge [REF yooj] *n.* a safe place or shelter from danger
 The abandoned kitten found <u>refuge</u> with the little boy.

resource [REE sawrs] *n.* something that can be drawn upon if needed
 The backpackers carried extra food as a <u>resource</u> in case the hike took longer than expected.

workhouses [WERK how ziz] *n.* poorhouses
 Long ago, paupers in England were sent to live in <u>workhouses</u>.

Unit 5 Resources: Drama
44

A Christmas Carol: Scrooge and Marley, *Act II* by Israel Horovitz
Vocabulary Warm-up Exercises

Exercise A *Fill in each blank in the paragraph below with an appropriate word from Word List A. Use each word only once.*

I can still [1] _____ the way my friend Sharon looked when she

would write a(n) [2] _____. At such a time, she had a faraway,

[3] _____ expression on her face. Of course, neither of us knew then

that Sharon would become a famous writer and earn a(n) [4] _____. I

remember the first time she read one of her works aloud to an audience. The

people [5] _____ enjoyed the reading. People continue to

[6] _____ her work to this day. Sharon has remained

[7] _____ by fame. To her, the [8] _____ of the words she

writes is that she is able to share her feelings with her readers.

Exercise B *Decide whether each statement below is* true *or* false. *Explain your answers.*

1. <u>Beggars</u> usually do not have enough to eat.
   T / F _____

2. If a person is caught stealing by the police, there will be a negative <u>consequence</u> for
   the thief's action.
   T / F _____

3. If we <u>preserved</u> the old photos, then we threw them out.
   T / F _____

4. If Brenda likes the perfume, she thinks it has an <u>odious</u> aroma.
   T / F _____

5. Most people do not like to be told what to do in a <u>nasty</u> way.
   T / F _____

6. If people are sent to <u>workhouses</u>, that means they have a lot of money.
   T / F _____

7. If we have no <u>refuge</u> from the storm, we have nowhere to go.
   T / F _____

8. It's good to have extra office supplies as a <u>resource</u> when we do a big project, so we
   do not run out of paper.
   T / F _____

Name _____ Date _____

A Christmas Carol: Scrooge and Marley, *Act II* by Israel Horovitz
Reading Warm-up A

Read the following passage. Pay special attention to the underlined words. Then, read it again, and complete the activities. Use a separate sheet of paper for your written answers.

Ebenezer Scrooge is the main character of the story *A Christmas Carol* by Charles Dickens. Scrooge is known for his mean spirit and miserliness. In the story, he is visited by three ghosts on Christmas Eve. Scrooge decides to change after he begins to <u>recollect</u> his past and to think about his future.

Scrooge is an important character in literature. This is shown by the effect he has had on our culture. Although the original story was written in 1843, it still inspires us today. Scrooge's name has come to mean a stingy soul who has a <u>fortune</u> in money but is not rich in spirit. Many a <u>poem</u> has been written that mentions Scrooge. Songs also have been written about him. Plays and movies, as well as musicals, have been created to retell the story of Scrooge. Certain cartoon characters also bear his name. *Scrooge* can even be found in the dictionary, defined as "a miserly, hardened person."

An important part of the story of Scrooge is his ability to change into a better person. When he realizes that few will ever miss him because of the sort of life he has lived, he becomes <u>thoughtful</u>. He begs for a chance to change. Scrooge does not want his life to remain <u>unaltered</u>. When he awakens on Christmas morning, he is determined to become a better person. He <u>heartily</u> celebrates the day. He brings good humor to all and generosity to those in need. Scrooge proves by his actions that he knows the <u>value</u> of sharing with others. In turn, those who know him change their opinion of him. They <u>praise</u> his generous actions. The story of Scrooge, though written long ago, continues to entertain and to teach us.

1. Circle the words that tell what Scrooge begins to <u>recollect</u>. What is a synonym for *recollect*?

2. Underline the words that tell what kind of <u>fortune</u> Scrooge had. What kind of *fortune* didn't he have?

3. Circle the word that tells what many a <u>poem</u> has mentioned. What is a *poem*?

4. Underline the words that tell why Scrooge becomes <u>thoughtful</u>. Use *thoughtful* in a sentence.

5. Circle the word that is an antonym for <u>unaltered</u>. What is something you would like to remain *unaltered*?

6. Underline the sentence that tells how Scrooge <u>heartily</u> celebrates Christmas day. Define *heartily*.

7. Underline the words that tell of what Scrooge shows he knows the <u>value</u>. Of what do you know the *value*?

8. Circle the words that tell what people <u>praise</u>. What is an antonym of *praise*?

Name _____ Date _____

Read the following passage. Pay special attention to the underlined words. Then, read it again, and complete the activities. Use a separate sheet of paper for your written answers.

During the mid-1800s in England, the Industrial Revolution took place. The possibility of finding jobs in factories in London caused many people to move there. The city's population rose by 450 percent at this time. Although some profited by the Industrial Revolution, many did not. The lower class and lower middle class suffered much poverty. A <u>consequence</u> of the increased population was the growth of more slums. Orphans often became <u>beggars</u> because the government had no laws to protect them.

Factory workers also had no labor laws to protect them at first. They were paid low wages. They worked long hours under conditions that were <u>odious</u> and unclean. Young children and women were seen by factory owners as an inexpensive labor <u>resource</u>. This was because they could be paid lower wages than men. Later laws were passed that <u>preserved</u> the rights of children. Unfortunately, these laws were very hard to enforce.

People who could not pay their debts were sent to prison, where they were kept with criminals. Later changes in the law provided that the poor be sent to <u>workhouses</u>. There the inmates provided labor to pay for their food and shelter. The conditions in the workhouses were often quite <u>nasty</u>. Many poor did not find the workhouses to be a proper <u>refuge</u> to escape their poverty. They preferred homeless lives in the city, begging for charity in order to survive.

Some of the charities that were set up to help the poor failed. One provided wage supplements to laborers who did not have enough money for food. This plan backfired. Employers lowered the wages of many workers because they knew their employees would still be able to get food by using the supplements.

The Industrial Revolution in England, although it stimulated the economy, also brought with it serious social problems that needed to be solved.

1. Underline the words that tell what the <u>consequence</u> of the increased population was. Define **consequence**.

2. Circle the words that tell why some orphans became <u>beggars</u>. Use **beggars** in a sentence.

3. Circle the word that tells more about how the conditions were <u>odious</u>. What is a synonym for **odious**?

4. Underline the words that tell why employers thought of women and children as a cheap labor <u>resource</u>. What does **resource** mean?

5. Underline the words that tell what the later laws <u>preserved</u>. Use **preserved** in a sentence.

6. Circle the words that tell who was sent to the <u>workhouses</u>. Explain how the **workhouses** were different from the prisons.

7. Underline the words that tell what was <u>nasty</u>. What is something you think is **nasty**?

8. Circle the words that tell who did not think the workhouses were a proper <u>refuge</u>. Define **refuge**.

"A Christmas Carol: Scrooge and Marley, *Act 2*" by Israel Horowitz

Writing About the Big Question

Do others see us more clearly than we see ourselves?

Big Question Vocabulary

appearance	appreciate	assumption	bias	characteristic
define	focus	identify	ignore	image
perception	perspective	reaction	reflect	reveal

A. *Choose one word from the list above to complete each sentence. There may be more than one right answer.*

1. Do you think someone's _____ can tell you something about their personality?

2. The players felt that the coach had a _____ against short players.

3. Luke found it difficult to _____ on his work in the noisy classroom.

B. *Follow the directions in responding to each of the items below.*

1. Make a list of four or more different ways people can communicate. For example, people can communicate by *telephone*. Write your response in a complete sentence.

   _____

   _____

2. Choose one of the means of communication you listed in question 1. Write three or more sentences describing the good and bad points of communicating that way. Use at least two of the Big Question vocabulary words. You may use the words in different forms (for example you can change *reflect* to *reflection*).

   _____

   _____

C. *Complete the sentence below. Then, write a short paragraph in which you connect this sentence to the big question.*

In order to change, we must first identify _____

_____

_____

Name _____   Date _____

A Christmas Carol: Scrooge and Marley, *Act II*, by Israel Horovitz
Reading: Adjust Your Reading Rate to Suit Your Purpose

Setting a purpose for reading is deciding before you read what you want to get out of a text. The purpose you set will affect the way you read.

Adjust your reading rate to suit your purpose. When you read a play, follow these guidelines:

- Read stage directions slowly and carefully. They describe action that may not be revealed by the dialogue.
- Read short lines of dialogue quickly in order to create the feeling of conversation.
- Read longer speeches by a single character slowly in order to reflect on the character's words and look for clues to the message.

DIRECTIONS: *Read the following passages, and answer the questions that follow each one.*

MAN # 1. Hey, you, watch where you're going.

MAN # 2. Watch it yourself, mate!

[PRESENT *sprinkles them directly, they change.*]

MAN # 1. I pray go in ahead of me. It's Christmas. You be first!

MAN # 2. No, no. I must insist that YOU be first!

1. How would you read the preceding dialogue? Why?

_____

2. How would you read the stage directions? Why?

_____

3. What important information do the stage directions contain? How does it affect your understanding of the lines that follow it?

_____

_____

PRESENT. Mark my words, Ebenezer Scrooge. I do not present the Cratchits to you because they are a handsome, or brilliant family. They are not handsome. They are not brilliant. They are not well-dressed, or tasteful to the times. Their shoes are not even waterproofed by virtue of money or cleverness spent. So when the pavement is wet, so are the insides of their shoes and the tops of their toes. They are the Cratchits, Mr. Scrooge. They are not highly special. They are happy, grateful, pleased with one another, contented with the time and how it passes. They don't sing very well, do they? But, nonetheless, they do sing . . . [*Pauses*] think of that, Scrooge. Fifteen shillings a week and they do sing . . . hear their song until its end.

4. How would you read the preceding passage? Why?

_____

_____

Name _____   Date _____

A Christmas Carol: Scrooge and Marley, *Act II,* by Israel Horovitz
Literary Analysis: Stage Directions

Stage directions are the words in the script of a drama that are not spoken by characters. When a play is performed, you can see the set, the characters, and the movements, and you can hear the sound effects. When you read a play, you get this information from the stage directions. Stage directions are usually printed in italic type and set off by brackets or parentheses.

DIRECTIONS: *Read the following passages, and answer the questions that follow each one.*

[BOB CRATCHIT *enters, carrying* TINY TIM *atop his shoulder. He wears a threadbare and fringe-less comforter hanging down in front of him.* TINY TIM *carries small crutches and his small legs are bound in an iron frame brace.*]

1. Who appears in this scene?

   _____

2. What does the description of Bob Cratchit reveal about the Cratchit family?

   _____

3. What does the description of Tiny Tim reveal about him?

   _____

   _____

SCROOGE. Specter, something informs me that our parting moment is at hand. I know it, but I know not how I know it.

[FUTURE *points to the other side of the stage. Lights out on* CRATCHITS. FUTURE *moves slowing, gliding . . .* FUTURE *points opposite.* FUTURE *leads* SCROOGE *to a wall and a tombstone. He points to the stone.*]

Am I that man those ghoulish parasites so gloated over?

4. Who appears in this scene? How do you know?

   _____

   _____

5. What do the stage directions reveal that the dialogue does not reveal?

   _____

   _____

   _____

A Christmas Carol: Scrooge and Marley, *Act II,* by Israel Horovitz
Vocabulary Builder

Word List

astonish   audible   compulsion   intercedes   meager   severe

A. DIRECTIONS: *Think about the meaning of the italicized word from the Word List in each sentence. Then, answer the question, and explain your answer.*

1. Scrooge's new attitude will *astonish* his family. Will they be surprised by it?

_____

2. Scrooge has a *compulsion* to go with each of the ghosts. Can he easily resist going?

_____

3. Mrs. Cratchit's judgment of Scrooge is *severe.* Does she think highly of him?

_____

4. Scrooge paid Cratchit a *meager* salary. Was the salary generous?

_____

5. The actor's voice is *audible* when he whispers. Can the audience hear him?

_____

6. The Ghost of Christmas Future *intercedes* on Scrooge's behalf. Does the ghost help Scrooge?

_____

B. WORD STUDY: *The Latin prefix* inter- *means "between, among." Read the following sentences. Use your knowledge of the prefix* inter- *to write a full sentence to answer each question. Include the italicized word in your answer.*

1. Have your parents ever *interceded* on your behalf?

_____

2. If a ball is *intercepted*, does it reach its destination?

_____

3. Is a highway *intersection* a place where two roads meet?

_____

Unit 5 Resources: Drama
51

Name _____   Date _____

A Christmas Carol: Scrooge and Marley, *Act II,* by Israel Horovitz
Enrichment: Holiday Observances

In Act II of *A Christmas Carol: Scrooge and Marley,* Scrooge observes how the Cratchits celebrate Christmas. Later in the play, he contributes to the Cratchits' celebration by sending the family a turkey, and he joins his nephew's family as they celebrate the holiday.

You and your family may observe and celebrate holidays throughout the year in special ways. Traditions may include festive meals, gift-giving, dressing in special clothing, visiting friends and relatives, or visiting special places.

A. DIRECTIONS: *Think of a holiday that is widely celebrated or observed. Think about all the special ways in which you, your family, and/or other people mark this occasion. Fill in details about the holiday observance.*

1. Name of holiday: _____

2. Meaning of holiday: _____

   _____

   _____

3. Clothing typically worn on holiday: _____

   _____

4. Special foods eaten on this holiday: _____

   _____

5. Places visited on this holiday: _____

   _____

6. Activities engaged in on this holiday: _____

   _____

7. Other traditions associated with this holiday: _____

   _____

B. DIRECTIONS: *Imagine that you could establish a new holiday. It might be serious (Help the Homeless Day) or lighthearted (Backwards Day). Answer these questions about your holiday:*

1. What is its name? _____

2. What is its purpose? _____

   _____

3. What traditions will your holiday involve? _____

   _____

Name _____   Date _____

A Christmas Carol: Scrooge and Marley, *Act II*, by Israel Horovitz
Integrated Language Skills: Grammar

Double Negatives

Double negatives occur when two negative words appear in a sentence, but only one is needed. Examples of negative words are *nothing, not, never,* and *no.* You can correct a double negative by revising the sentence.

Incorrect	Correct
I do <u>not</u> have <u>no</u> homework tonight.	I do <u>not</u> have <u>any</u> homework tonight.
You <u>never</u> said <u>nothing</u> about that movie.	You <u>never</u> said <u>anything</u> about that movie.

A. DIRECTIONS: *Put a checkmark (✓) next to each sentence that uses a negative word correctly. Put an ✗ next to each sentence that contains a double negative.*

____ 1. Do not ever say nothing to Mom about the surprise party.

____ 2. You never told me anything about your new coach.

____ 3. The team never had time to make a comeback.

____ 4. We do not have no reason to get up early tomorrow.

____ 5. They did not have no money for the movie.

B. Writing Application: *Rewrite each sentence to eliminate the double negative.*

1. We do not have no bread for sandwiches.

_____

2. The spy never had no intention of giving himself up.

_____

3. This article does not have nothing to do with our assignment.

_____

4. They are not going to no championship game tonight.

_____

5. Our dog will not ever eat no food she does not like.

_____

53

A Christmas Carol: Scrooge and Marley, *Act II,* by Israel Horovitz
Integrated Language Skills: Support for Writing a Tribute

To prepare to write a **tribute,** or an expression of admiration, to the changed Ebenezer Scrooge, answer the following questions.

What is Scrooge like before the change?

_____

_____

What anecdotes—brief stories that make a point—illustrate Scrooge's character before the change?

_____

_____

_____

_____

What causes Scrooge to change?

_____

_____

_____

What is Scrooge like after the change?

_____

_____

What anecdotes illustrate Scrooge's character after the change?

_____

_____

_____

_____

Now, write a draft of your tribute to Scrooge. Be sure to explain how Scrooge has changed and why his new behavior deserves to be honored. Use this space to write your first draft.

_____

_____

_____

_____

A Christmas Carol: Scrooge and Marley, *Act II*, by Israel Horovitz
Integrated Language Skills: Support for Extend Your Learning

Listening and Speaking

You must base your **dramatic monologue** on Scrooge's thoughts as he interacts with the Ghost of Christmas Present or the Ghost of Christmas Past. As you prepare your monologue, answer these questions:

On which scene and with which ghost will you focus your monologue? (Be specific.)

_____

What is happening in this scene? _____

_____

What is Scrooge feeling in this scene? Is he excited, eager, anxious, frightened?

_____

Now, write a draft of your monologue. Remember to speak as if you were Scrooge: Use the pronouns *I, me, my, mine,* and *myself.* Practice presenting the monologue, and then revise your draft to correct any weaknesses you notice.

_____

_____

_____

_____

_____

_____

_____

_____

_____

_____

_____

_____

_____

_____

_____

Name _____ Date _____

A Christmas Carol: Scrooge and Marley, *Act II,* by Israel Horovitz
Open-Book Test

Short Answer *Write your responses to the questions in this section on the lines provided.*

1. How can you tell this passage from the middle of Act II, Scene 1, of *A Christmas Carol: Scrooge and Marley* is stage directions? What does it mainly describe?

    [*PRESENT is wearing a simple green robe. The walls around the room are now covered in greenery, as well. The room seems to be a perfect grove now: leaves of holly, mistletoe, and ivy reflect the stage lights. . . .*]

    _____

    _____

2. At the end of Act II, Scene 1, of *A Christmas Carol: Scrooge and Marley*, Scrooge says, "Tonight, if you have aught to teach me, let me profit by it." What is Scrooge asking The Ghost of Christmas Present to do? How does this tell you that Scrooge is changing?

    _____

    _____

3. In the stage directions found near the beginning of Act II, Scene 2, of *A Christmas Carol: Scrooge and Marley*, playwright Israel Horovitz gives these stage directions:

    [*. . . They will, perhaps, sing about being poor at Christmastime, whatever.*]

    Why do you think the playwright wrote these directions?

    _____

    _____

4. Your reading rate changes depending on whether you are reading stage directions, dialogue, or longer speeches. How would you read Bob Cratchit's description of Tiny Tim in the middle of *A Christmas Carol: Scrooge and Marley*, Act II, Scene 3? The speech begins, "As good as gold, and even better." Explain.

    _____

    _____

5. Explain the reading rate that is best suited for the passage in the middle of Act II, Scene 3, of *A Christmas Carol: Scrooge and Marley*. In the passage, Scrooge and The Ghost of Christmas Present are talking. The passage begins with Scrooge saying, "Spirit, tell me if Tiny Tim will live."

    _____

    _____

6. In the first half of Act II, Scene 4, of *A Christmas Carol: Scrooge and Marley*, Scrooge wants to be audible to his nephew and niece. What might have happened if he were audible? Base your answer on the meaning of *audible*.

    _____

    _____

7. In the middle of Act II, Scene 4, of *A Christmas Carol: Scrooge and Marley*, Scrooge and The Ghost of Christmas Future watch as three people go through the contents of a house. Scrooge tells the Spirit, "this is a fearful place. In leaving it, I shall not leave its lesson, trust me." What does Scrooge mean? Explain.

_____

_____

_____

8. In the beginning of Act II, Scene 5, of *A Christmas Carol: Scrooge and Marley*, Scrooge awakens after his journey with The Ghost of Christmas Future. Scrooge says to Marley, ". . . the shadows of things that would have been, may now be dispelled." What does Scrooge mean?

_____

_____

_____

9. At the end of Act II, Scene 5, of *A Christmas Carol: Scrooge and Marley*, Marley says to the audience that Scrooge "knew how to keep Christmas well." What new traits has the character Scrooge acquired? Why are these traits important to the story?

_____

_____

_____

10. In the chart below, write the important information the reader gets from each set of stage directions from Act II of *A Christmas Carol: Scrooge and Marley*. Then, answer the question that follows the chart.

Stage Directions	Important Information
Scene 1: [*Heaped up on the floor, to form a kind of throne, are turkeys, geese, game, poultry, brawn, great joints of meat, . . .*]	
Scene 3: [*Tiny Tim . . . wears a threadbare and fringeless comforter hanging down in front of him.*]	
Scene 5: [*Scrooge goes to him and embraces him.*]	

Which of the above is a stage direction for actor movement? Which actor is moving?

_____

Essay

Write an extended response to the question of your choice or to the question or questions your teacher assigns you.

11. Why is The Ghost of Christmas Future the most frightening of the three ghosts in *A Christmas Carol: Scrooge and Marley*? In an essay, explain what is frightening about this character. Cite two details from the play to support your answer.

12. Tiny Tim's character is revealed through stage directions and dialogue. In an essay, describe the boy based on what you learn in Act II, Scenes 3, 4, and 5 of *A Christmas Carol: Scrooge and Marley*. Tell what Tiny Tim looks like, how he feels about his family, and any other information about him that is revealed in the play you read. If Tiny Tim could be said to represent a single characteristic, what would it be?

13. Act II of *A Christmas Carol: Scrooge and Marley* contains several messages. In an essay, tell how two of the following messages are conveyed:

    • When one person changes for the better, others are affected for the better.
    • Only greedy people will be present at the end of a greedy life.
    • Wealth makes people rich only if they share their wealth.

    Include at least two details from the play to support your points.

14. **Thinking About the Big Question: Do others see us more clearly than we see ourselves?** In Act II, Scenes 3 and 4, of *A Christmas Carol: Scrooge and Marley*, Scrooge visits the Cratchits and his nephew and niece. They each see him in a different way. In an essay, describe how the Cratchits and Fred and his wife see Scrooge. Which character, if any, sees him most clearly and accurately? Use details from the play to support your answer.

Oral Response

15. Go back to question 2, 7, or 9 or to the question your teacher assigns you. Take a few minutes to expand your answer and prepare an oral response. Find additional details in Act II of *A Christmas Carol: Scrooge and Marley* that support your points. If necessary, make notes to guide your oral response.

A Christmas Carol: Scrooge and Marley, *Act II,* by Israel Horovitz
Selection Test A

Critical Reading *Identify the letter of the choice that best answers the question.*

____ 1. What is mainly described in this passage from Act II, Scene 1, of *A Christmas Carol: Scrooge and Marley*?

> [PRESENT *is wearing a simple green robe. The walls around the room are now covered in greenery, as well. The room seems to be a perfect grove now: leaves of holly, mistletoe and ivy reflect the stage lights. Suddenly, there is a mighty roar of flame in the fireplace and now the hearth burns with a lavish, warming fire.*]

A. the Ghost's size

B. the Ghost's room

C. the Ghost's attitude

D. the Ghost's orchard

____ 2. When he meets the Ghost of Christmas Present in Act II, Scene 1, what does Scrooge say that shows he has already changed?

A. "Come in, come in! Come in and know me better!"

B. "Have you had many brothers, Spirit?"

C. "A tremendous family to provide for!"

D. "If you have aught to teach me, let me profit by it."

____ 3. What element of drama is shown in this excerpt from *A Christmas Carol: Scrooge and Marley*, Act II, Scene 1?

> [SCROOGE *walks cautiously to* PRESENT *and touches his robe. When he does, lightning flashes, thunder claps, music plays. Blackout*]

A. dialogue

B. plot

C. stage directions

D. setting

____ 4. What do you learn about Scrooge from this passage from Act II, Scene 3?

> PRESENT. This is the home of your employee, Mr. Scrooge. Don't you know it?
> SCROOGE. Do you mean Cratchit, Spirit? Do you mean this is Cratchit's home?

A. He has a poor memory for places.

B. He has forgotten his employee's name.

C. He has never visited the Cratchits' home.

D. He is trying to annoy the Ghost.

_____ 5. In Act II, Scene 3, of *A Christmas Carol: Scrooge and Marley*, what is Scrooge's first reaction on seeing Cratchit's family?

A. He thinks Cratchit has too many children.

B. He is afraid that Tiny Tim will not live.

C. He is touched that Cratchit toasts him.

D. He wants to think about what he sees.

_____ 6. In Act II, Scene 3, of *A Christmas Carol: Scrooge and Marley*, what does Christmas Present say to indicate that Scrooge's actions can affect the outcome of events?

A. "I would say that he gets the pleasure of his family."

B. "I see a vacant seat . . . in the poor chimney corner, and a crutch without an owner."

C. "If these shadows remain unaltered by the future, the child will die."

D. "Save your breath, Mr. Scrooge. You can't be seen or heard."

_____ 7. If you were to adjust your reading rate to suit your purpose, how would you read this passage from *A Christmas Carol: Scrooge and Marley*, Act II, Scene 3?

MRS. CRATCHIT. And how did little Tim behave?

BOB. As good as gold, and even better. Somehow he gets thoughtful sitting by himself so much, and thinks the strangest things you ever heard. He told me, coming home, that he hoped people saw him in the church, because he was a cripple, and it might be pleasant to them to remember upon Christmas Day, who made lame beggars walk and blind men see. . . . He has the oddest ideas sometimes, but he seems all the while to be growing stronger and more hearty . . . one would never know.

A. slowly, to look for clues to the message

B. quickly, to create a feeling of conversation

C. quickly, to pass over unimportant information

D. slowly, to look for information not in the dialogue

_____ 8. In Act II, Scene 4, of *A Christmas Carol: Scrooge and Marley*, what are the two women and the man selling to Old Joe?

A. items they stole from Scrooge's rooms after he died

B. items Scrooge gave them before he died

C. items Cratchit gave them after Scrooge died

D. items Scrooge kept to remind himself of his first love

_____ 9. In Act II, Scene 4, of *A Christmas Carol: Scrooge and Marley*, what does the Ghost of Christmas Future do that gives Scrooge hope?

A. He never speaks a word to Scrooge.

B. He points to Scrooge's tombstone.

C. He pulls away from Scrooge.

D. He drops his garments and disappears.

___ **10.** If you were adjusting your reading rate to suit your purpose, how would you read this passage from Act II, Scene 5?

> SCROOGE. . . . I am light as a feather, I am happy as an angel, I am as merry as a schoolboy. [*Yells out window and then out to audience*] Merry Christmas to everybody! Merry Christmas to everybody! A Happy New Year to all the world! Hallo there! Whoop! Whoop! Hallo! Hallo!

   A. slowly and carefully

   B. quickly, to create the feeling of conversation

   C. quickly, skipping the stage directions

   D. slowly, to look for clues to the message

Vocabulary and Grammar

___ **11.** In which line is the opposite of the word *audible* best expressed?

   A. "Spirit, tell me if Tiny Tim will live."

   B. "Save your breath, Mr. Scrooge. You can't be . . . heard."

   C. "I'll drink to his health for your sake . . . , but not for his sake."

   D. "Mark my words, Ebenezer Scrooge."

___ **12.** Which of the following sentences contains a double negative?

   A. No one is as dearly loved as Tiny Tim.

   B. The man does not know much about Scrooge's death.

   C. Scrooge declares that he is not the man he was.

   D. Scrooge realizes that he has not missed nothing.

Essay

13. In Act II of *A Christmas Carol: Scrooge and Marley*, Scrooge visits the homes of the Cratchits and his nephew, Fred, with the Ghost of Christmas Present. In an essay, describe what those two visits have in common and what Scrooge learns from them.

14. Why is the Ghost of Christmas Future the most frightening of the three ghosts in *A Christmas Carol: Scrooge and Marley*? In an essay, explain what is frightening about this character. Cite two details from the play to support your points.

15. Thinking About the Big Question: Do others see us more clearly than we see ourselves? In Act II, Scenes 3 and 4, of *A Christmas Carol: Scrooge and Marley*, Scrooge visits the Cratchits and his nephew and niece. They each see him in a different way. In an essay, describe how the Cratchits and Fred and his wife see Scrooge. Use details from the play to support your answer.

A Christmas Carol: Scrooge and Marley, *Act II,* by Israel Horovitz
Selection Test B

Critical Reading *Identify the letter of the choice that best completes the statement or answers the question.*

____ 1. In Act II, Scene 1, of *A Christmas Carol: Scrooge and Marley*, Marley says that nothing will astonish Scrooge now and so he will give him nothing. What does he mean by that?
  A. He wants to drive Scrooge crazy.
  B. He is making a play on the word *nothing.*
  C. He has used all his magic tricks in the first act.
  D. He is afraid Scrooge will discover how he does his magic.

____ 2. What is the most important information the reader gets from these stage directions in Act II, Scene 1, of *A Christmas Carol: Scrooge and Marley*?
  [*Heaped up on the floor, to form a kind of throne, are turkeys, geese, game, poultry, brawn, great joints of meat, . . . mince-pies, plum puddings, . . . cherry-cheeked apples, juicy oranges, luscious pears, . . . and seething bowls of punch, that make the chamber dim with their delicious steam. Upon this throne sits* PRESENT, *glorious to see.*]
  A. how the Ghost of Christmas Present looks
  B. how the Ghost of Christmas Present spends his time
  C. what foods wealthy people ate in nineteenth-century England
  D. how a room full of food and drink might look and smell

____ 3. What does the playwright most likely mean to suggest at the end of these stage directions from Act II, Scene 2, of *A Christmas Carol: Scrooge and Marley*?
  [*The choral groups will hum the song they have just completed now and mill about the streets, carrying their dinners to the bakers' shops and restaurants. They will, perhaps, sing about being poor at Christmastime, whatever.*]
  A. The chorus should continue singing and carrying food.
  B. The chorus members should be grouped together on the stage.
  C. The director should decide what the chorus will sing about.
  D. The bakers' shops and the restaurants should be open for business.

____ 4. If you were to adjust your reading rate to suit your purpose, how would you best read this passage from Act II, Scene 3, of *A Christmas Carol: Scrooge and Marley*?
  SCROOGE. What is this place, Spirit?
  PRESENT. This is the home of your employee, Mr. Scrooge. Don't you know it?
  SCROOGE. Do you mean Cratchit, Spirit? Do you mean this is Cratchit's home?
  A. slowly, to look for clues to the message
  B. quickly, to create a feeling of conversation
  C. quickly, to get a general sense of the conversation
  D. slowly, to look for information that is not stated directly

_____ 5. What purpose is served by these stage directions from Act II, Scene 3?

> [SCROOGE *touches* PRESENT'S *robe. The lights fade out on the* CRATCHITS, *who sit, frozen, at the table.* SCROOGE *and* PRESENT *in a spotlight now. Thunder, lightning, smoke. They are gone.*]

    A. They explain Scrooge's character.
    B. They signal a change of setting.
    C. They describe the Cratchit home.
    D. They show the director's skill.

_____ 6. What aspect of this passage, from Act II, Scene 4, of *A Christmas Carol: Scrooge and Marley*, signals that it should be read slowly?

> PRESENT. They are Man's children, and they cling to me, appealing from their fathers. The boy is Ignorance; the girl is Want. Beware them both, and all of their degree, but most of all beware this boy, for I see that written on his brow which is doom, unless the writing be erased.

    A. It takes place in Act II of the play.
    B. It contains no stage directions.
    C. It is a longer speech by one character.
    D. It is conversational in tone.

_____ 7. According to Act II, Scene 4, of *A Christmas Carol: Scrooge and Marley*, why does Fred intend to invite Scrooge to Christmas dinner every year?
    A. Scrooge reminds Fred of his mother, Scrooge's sister.
    B. Fred likes to tease Scrooge and make him angry.
    C. Fred and his wife enjoy laughing at their miserly uncle.
    D. Fred wants Scrooge to see how meager their Christmas is.

_____ 8. What does Scrooge mean by this line from Act II, Scene 4?

> Spirit, this is a fearful place. In leaving it, I shall not leave its lesson, trust me. Let us go!

    A. I am afraid and want us to leave.
    B. This is not a good place for a school.
    C. I will not forget the lesson I learned here.
    D. If you do not trust me, I will not follow you.

_____ 9. Why do the scoundrels in Act II, Scene 4, of *A Christmas Carol: Scrooge and Marley* have access to Scrooge's possessions?
    A. Scrooge died alone with no one to take care of his things.
    B. Scrooge left his things to anyone who might need them.
    C. Scrooge did not get around to making a will before he died.
    D. Scrooge left his door unlocked on the last night he was alive.

_____ 10. Which line spoken by Marley in Act II of *A Christmas Carol: Scrooge and Marley* best summarizes the theme of the play?
    A. "The firm of Scrooge and Marley is doubly blessed."
    B. "Yes, Ebenezer, the bedpost is your own. Believe it!"
    C. "Scrooge was better than his word. He did it all and infinitely more."
    D. "And it was always said of him that he knew how to keep Christmas well."

Vocabulary and Grammar

____ 11. In which line is the meaning of the word *astonish* expressed?
A. Marley says that nothing will surprise Scrooge, given all that he has seen.
B. Christmas Present asks Scrooge whether he has ever before seen anyone like him.
C. Fred's wife expresses her pleasure at the amount of laughter in her marriage.
D. Bob Cratchit requests that Martha play the notes on the lute for Tiny Tim's song.

____ 12. In which sentence is the meaning of the word *severe* expressed?
A. On Christmas Day, the streets are full of people going to work in the homes of the rich.
B. Christmas Present seems to scold Scrooge for not recognizing the Cratchits' home.
C. Scrooge wonders aloud whether he can affect the events of the future.
D. When the weather is harsh, people make music to lift their spirits.

____ 13. Which sentence does *not* contain a double negative?
A. Mrs. Cratchit does not want to make no toast to Scrooge.
B. No one says nothing about the cause of Scrooge's death.
C. Cratchit says they will not never quarrel among themselves.
D. Scrooge seems to want to know nothing about his death.

Essay

14. Act II of *A Christmas Carol: Scrooge and Marley* contains several messages. In an essay, tell how one of these messages is conveyed in the second act of the play:

• When one person changes for the better, others are affected for the better.
• Only greedy people will be present at the end of a greedy life.
• Wealth makes people rich only if they share their wealth.

Include at least two details from the play to support your points.

15. Tiny Tim's character is revealed through stage directions and dialogue. In an essay, describe the boy based on what you learn in Act II of *A Christmas Carol: Scrooge and Marley*. Tell what he looks like, how he feels about his family, and any other information about him that is revealed in the text you read. If Tiny Tim could be said to represent a single characteristic, what would it be?

16. **Thinking About the Big Question: Do others see us more clearly than we see ourselves?** In Act II, Scenes 3 and 4, of *A Christmas Carol: Scrooge and Marley*, Scrooge visits the Cratchits and his nephew and niece. They each see him in a different way. In an essay, describe how the Cratchits and Fred and his wife see Scrooge. Which character, if any, sees him most clearly and accurately? Use details from the play to support your answer.

Vocabulary Warm-up Word Lists

Study these words from the play. Then, complete the activities.

Word List A

absolute [AB suh loot] *adj.* complete or whole
After the stirring speech, there was <u>absolute</u> silence.

compete [kuhm PEET] *v.* to contend or to vie for something
The county ski teams will <u>compete</u> for a downhill racing prize.

enormously [ee NOOR muhs lee] *adv.* immensely
The <u>enormously</u> big wedding cake took up the whole table.

faintly [FAYNT lee] *adv.* weakly or slightly
Anna <u>faintly</u> heard a noise outside the door.

feast [FEEST] *n.* big, festive meal
We ate a huge <u>feast</u> at the anniversary party.

grace [GRAYS] *n.* sense of what is right, proper, and decent
The host greeted his guests with a welcome that was full of <u>grace</u>.

gratitude [GRAT i tood] *n.* thankfulness
The winning team felt a sense of <u>gratitude</u> for their coach.

suitors [SOOT erz] *n.* men who are courting a woman
Linda's <u>suitors</u> called her each day.

Word List B

apprentices [uh PREN tis iz] *n.* people who work to learn a trade from an expert
The silversmith's <u>apprentices</u> were eager to learn how to work with metal.

attention [uh TEN shuhn] *n.* the state of standing tall, awaiting an order or instruction
The soldiers stood at <u>attention</u> when the commander entered the room.

bound [BOWND] *adv.* certain, sure, or having one's mind made up
We are <u>bound</u> to win this tournament.

convenient [kuhn VEEN yuhnt] *adj.* causing little trouble or work
Will it be <u>convenient</u> for you if we meet at eight o'clock?

dignity [DIG ni tee] *n.* the quality of being worthy of honor or respect
Susan had a lot of <u>dignity</u> when she addressed the court.

master [MAS ter] *n.* boss or person in charge
The <u>master</u> of the shop told his employees to be on time.

snuffs [SNUHFS] *v.* puts out a candle or extinguishes something
The priest <u>snuffs</u> out the candles after the service.

wages [WAYJ iz] *n.* pay
Dan spent his week's <u>wages</u> on repairing his car.

from A Christmas Carol: Scrooge and Marley, *Act I, Scenes 2 & 5* by Israel Horovitz
Vocabulary Warm-up Exercises

Exercise A *Fill in each blank in the paragraph below with an appropriate word from Word List A. Use each word only once.*

Rachel was a very nice person and was [1] _____ popular with her classmates. At the holiday [2] _____ at school, aside from lots of food, there was also music for dancing. Rachel had many [3] _____ . Each wished to [4] _____ for a chance to dance with Rachel. She responded to each one with complete and [5] _____ politeness. Her thankfulness was not [6] _____ expressed. Instead, she treated her admirers with dignified [7] _____ , showing [8] _____ for each invitation she received.

Exercise B *Answer the questions with complete sentences.*

1. Would <u>apprentices</u> be likely to earn a lot of money?

   _____

2. If it is <u>convenient</u> to get to work, does it take an extremely long time?

   _____

3. If we are <u>bound</u> to run into a snowstorm, should we allow some extra travel time?

   _____

4. When someone stands at <u>attention</u>, is he or she likely to be a member of the armed forces?

   _____

5. Do most people dislike being treated with <u>dignity</u>?

   _____

6. If the craftsperson is a <u>master</u> at woodworking, is she or he probably just learning that trade?

   _____

7. If the girl <u>snuffs</u> out the flame, will the room probably grow darker?

   _____

8. Will a person be likely to earn more <u>wages</u> if he or she spends more time working?

   _____

Name _____   Date _____

from A Christmas Carol: Scrooge and Marley, *Act I, Scenes 2 & 5* by Israel Horovitz
Reading Warm-up A

Read the following passage. Pay special attention to the underlined words. Then, read it again, and complete the activities. Use a separate sheet of paper for your written answers.

December 22, 1843

Dear Diary,

Today was a wonderful day! My family and I went to my Aunt Annie's for a holiday party. It was an <u>absolute</u> success! Cousin Mary played the piano as we danced to her lively tunes. Some dancers moved with a sense of <u>grace</u>, while others, such as my brothers, tried to <u>compete</u> with each other to see how many high kicks, fancy steps, and turns they could do!

My older sister Julianne had many <u>suitors</u>. They stood by her side as they awaited a turn to dance with her. I noticed she did not go anywhere near the kissing ball, which was hanging from the ceiling of the room. It was filled with mistletoe and other evergreens. Everyone knows that if you are found beneath it, you must kiss someone.

We enjoyed a fine <u>feast</u> of goose and beef. The tasty treats were <u>enormously</u> popular with all. On Christmas, I look forward to more holiday foods, for that is when we will eat our delicious plum pudding. It is made of prunes, raisins, and beef. Sweet mince pies will also be served. They are made of spices, fruit, and mincemeat. We will eat them throughout the twelve days of Christmas in order to bring us twelve months of good luck in the coming year.

Aunt Annie's house looked lovely. It was decorated with fresh evergreen boughs, which are thought to bring good luck and to represent renewed life. The entire family sang carols, and it was not <u>faintly</u> done. I believe our booming voices could be heard near and far.

I was sad to see the evening come to an end, for it was such fun. I hugged my aunt, expressing my <u>gratitude</u> for having such a fine family with whom to celebrate! Well, that is all for tonight.

Nora

1. Circle the words that tell what was an <u>absolute</u> success. What does *absolute* mean?

2. Underline the words that tell who moved with <u>grace</u>. Use *grace* in a sentence.

3. Circle the words that describe how Nora's brothers tried to <u>compete</u>. What other things can people *compete* in?

4. Underline the words that tell what Julianne's <u>suitors</u> did. Define *suitors*.

5. Circle the words that tell of what the <u>feast</u> consisted. To you, what foods make up a *feast*?

6. Underline the words that tell what was <u>enormously</u> popular. What is a synonym for *enormously*?

7. Underline the words that tell what was not <u>faintly</u> done. Describe how it must have sounded.

8. Circle the words that tell for what Nora was expressing her <u>gratitude</u>. Define *gratitude*.

Unit 5 Resources: Drama

Name _____ Date _____

from **A Christmas Carol: Scrooge and Marley,** *Act I,* **Scenes 2 & 5** by Israel Horovitz
Reading Warm-up B

Read the following passage. Pay special attention to the underlined words. Then, read it again, and complete the activities. Use a separate sheet of paper for your written answers.

The Victorian age in Britain was named after the ruling queen of the time, Victoria. It took place during the 1800s. At that time, families who could not pay their debts were sent to places called workhouses.

The children in workhouses were often given jobs to help pay off their families' debts. Factory owners and craftspeople looking for cheap labor knew they were <u>bound</u> to find such workers among poor children. Such employers found it <u>convenient</u> to ask the workhouses to give them youngsters as <u>apprentices</u>.

If a child became an apprentice, he or she would learn a trade, such as blacksmith or glass blower. The child would be given room and board in exchange for working for a <u>master</u>, the owner or boss of the shop. If a child was being apprenticed, indenture papers were drawn up. These papers were a contract between the master and the apprentice. It listed the conditions under which the apprentice would work. It also told how long the arrangement would last. One such contract describes the apprenticeship of a boy of thirteen who was sent to work with a shoemaker for seven years. The boy would not receive any pay, or <u>wages</u>, for the first four years. Every year after that he would receive a small amount of money.

Some masters were kind and treated the young workers with respect and <u>dignity</u>. Others saw the youngsters as slaves. These apprentices needed always to be at <u>attention</u>, ready to perform the next task required of them. In such cases, the youngsters' spirit was extinguished, just as one <u>snuffs</u> out a candle's flame.

Some workhouses looked into the conditions that the children would be working under during their apprenticeships. They wanted to make sure that the work was not too difficult and that the youngsters would be treated well. Unfortunately, those workhouses were the exception, not the rule. Thus, the lives of many young apprentices were not easy.

1. Underline the words that tell what the factory owners and craftspeople were <u>bound</u> to find among the poor children. Define *bound*.

2. Circle the words that tell what the employers found to be <u>convenient</u>. Use *convenient* in a sentence.

3. Circle the sentences that define what <u>apprentices</u> are. If you were an *apprentice*, what craft would you like to learn to do?

4. Underline the words that tell what a <u>master</u> is. Use *master* in a sentence.

5. Underline the word that is a synonym for <u>wages</u>. Do you think it was fair that the boy would receive no *wages* for the first four years?

6. Circle the words that describe the condition of being treated with <u>dignity</u>. Define *dignity*.

7. Underline the words that tell more about how the apprentices who had to be at <u>attention</u> needed to act. Who else might need to stand at *attention*?

8. Circle the words that compare something to the way one <u>snuffs</u> out a candle. Define *snuffs*.

Name _____ Date _____

from **A Christmas Carol: Scrooge and Marley,** *Act I, Scenes 2 & 5* by Israel Horovitz

Writing About the Big Question

Do others see us more clearly than we see ourselves?

Big Question Vocabulary

appearance	appreciate	assumption	bias	characteristic
define	focus	identify	ignore	image
perception	perspective	reaction	reflect	reveal

A. *Choose one word from the list above to complete each sentence. There may be more than one right answer.*

1. The wrong _____ will lead to the wrong conclusion.

2. It is important to _____ on life's big events.

3. Her family members tried not to _____ the plans for the surprise party.

B. *Follow the directions in responding to each of the items below.*

1. Think of at least three adjectives or descriptive phrases that you feel describe you well. List the adjectives or phrases in a complete sentence.

   _____

   _____

2. Write at least two sentences describing an article of clothing that makes you feel special. Write your response in complete sentences. Use at least one of the Big Question vocabulary words. You may use the words in different forms (for example, may can change *reveal* to *reveals*).

   _____

   _____

C. *Complete the sentence below. Then, write a short paragraph in which you connect this sentence to the big question.*

Over time, people change _____

_____

_____

from **A Christmas Carol: Scrooge and Marley,** *Act I, Scenes 2 & 5* by Israel Horovitz
Literary Analysis: Comparing Characters

A **character** is a person who takes part in a literary work. Like main characters in stories and novels, main characters in dramas, have traits that make them unique. These may include qualities such as dependability, intelligence, selfishness, and stubbornness. The characters in dramas have motives, or reasons, for behaving the way they do. For example, one character may be motivated by compassion, while another may be motivated by guilt.

When you read a drama, pay attention to what each character says and does, and note the reactions those words and actions spark in others. Notice what those words and actions reveal about the character's traits and motives.

In drama, one way to develop a character is through a **foil,** a character whose behavior and attitude contrast with those of the main character. With a foil, audiences can see good in contrast with bad or generousness in contrast with selfishness.

DIRECTIONS: *Answer the following questions to compare the older Scrooge with Fezziwig.*

Question	Scrooge	Fezziwig
1. What does the character say?		
2. What does the character do?		
3. How does the character react to Christmas?		
4. What do other characters say to or about him?		
5. What adjectives describe the character?		

from A Christmas Carol: Scrooge and Marley, *Act I, Scenes 2 & 5* by Israel Horovitz
Vocabulary Builder

Word List

fiddler   snuffs   suitors

A. DIRECTIONS: *Complete the word maps by writing a definition, synonyms, and an example sentence for each word from the Word List.*

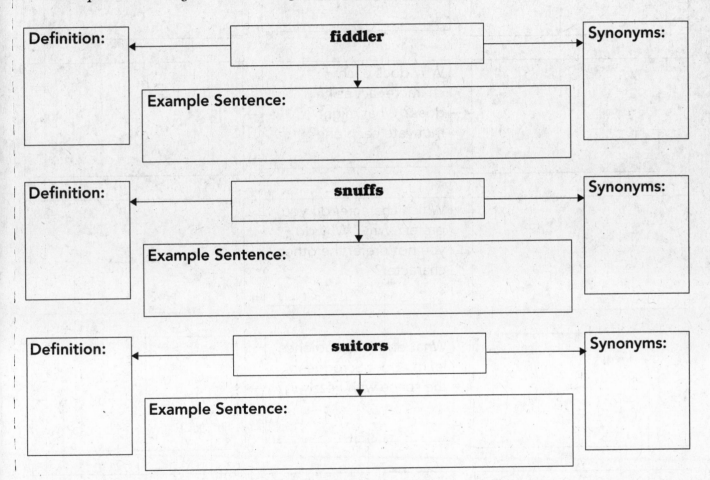

B. DIRECTIONS: *Write the letter of the word whose meaning is* most like *that of the word from the Word List.*

_____ 1. fiddler
   A. crab   **B.** musician   **C.** violinist   **D.** tinkerer

_____ 2. snuffs
   A. sniffs   **B.** erases   **C.** blots   **D.** extinguishes

_____ 3. suitors
   A. boyfriends   **B.** tailors   **C.** lawyers   **D.** apprentices

Name _____ Date _____

from **A Christmas Carol: Scrooge and Marley,** *Act I, Scenes 2 & 5* by Israel Horovitz
Support for Writing to Compare Literary Works

Use this graphic organizer to gather notes for an essay in which you compare and contrast Fezziwig and Scrooge.

Scrooge   **Fezziwig**

	How does each character behave? Think about what each one says and does.	

	Why does each character act as he does? What might motivate each one?	

	Which character do you prefer? Why? Why do you not prefer the other character?	

	What does the audience learn about Scrooge in the scene with Fezziwig?	

	How does Fezziwig help Scrooge change?	

Now, use your notes to write an essay comparing and contrasting Fezziwig and Scrooge. Be sure to discuss how each character's actions and words help the playwright make a point about Scrooge and his behavior.

Name _____   Date _____

Open-Book Test

Short Answer *Write your responses to the questions in this section on the lines provided.*

1. Before he leaves for the evening in Act I, Scene 2, of *A Christmas Carol: Scrooge and Marley,* Cratchit snuffs out his candle. Why does he do this? Base your answer on the meaning of *snuffs.*

   _____

   _____

   _____

2. In Act I, Scene 2, of *A Christmas Carol: Scrooge and Marley,* Cratchit rushes away after he says, "Merry Christmas, Mr. Scrooge." Why does he leave in such a hurry?

   _____

   _____

   _____

3. According to Act I, Scene 2, of *A Christmas Carol: Scrooge and Marley,* Scrooge objects when people enjoy Christmas. Why does he react this way? What does it tell you about his character?

   _____

   _____

   _____

4. In Act I, Scene 5, of *A Christmas Carol: Scrooge and Marley,* how does Fezziwig feel about Christmas? What details tell you how he feels?

   _____

   _____

   _____

5. In Act I, Scene 5, of *A Christmas Carol: Scrooge and Marley,* why are the suitors following Fezziwig's daughters? Base your answer on the meaning of *suitors.*

   _____

   _____

   _____

6. How does Fezziwig treat others in Act I, Scene 5, of *A Christmas Carol: Scrooge and Marley.* How is it different from Scrooge's treatment of others in Scene 2?

   _____

   _____

   _____

7. In Act I, Scene 5, of *A Christmas Carol: Scrooge and Marley*, how do Young Ebenezer and Dick Wilkins feel about Fezziwig? What qualities does Fezziwig have that make them feel that way?

_____

_____

_____

_____

8. In Act I, Scene 5, of *A Christmas Carol: Scrooge and Marley*, Young Ebenezer says that if he ever owned his own firm, he would treat his employees "with the same dignity and the same grace" as Fezziwig does. Does this statement surprise you?

_____

_____

_____

_____

9. A *foil* is a character who is contrasted with another character to help develop that character. In what way is Fezziwig in Act I, Scene 5, of *A Christmas Carol: Scrooge and Marley* a foil for Scrooge in Act I, Scene 2?

_____

_____

_____

_____

10. In the chart below, write two qualities that these characters in *A Christmas Carol: Scrooge and Marley* possess. Then, answer the question that follows the chart.

Character	Qualities
Young Ebenezer	
Bob Cratchit	
Fezziwig	

Which character, or foil, do you think contrasts the most with the character of the older Scrooge in Act I, Scene 2? Explain.

_____

_____

_____

Essay

Write an extended response to the question of your choice or to the question or questions your teacher assigns you.

11. Ebenezer Scrooge and Fezziwig both own businesses. In an essay, describe them both as bosses. How do they treat their employees? What do others think of them? Would you want to work for either of them? Why or why not? Cite details from Act I, Scenes 2 and 5, of *A Christmas Carol: Scrooge and Marley* to support your response.

12. The brief dialogue between Scrooge and Cratchit in Act I, Scene 2, of *A Christmas Carol: Scrooge and Marley* tells a great deal about both men's characters. In an essay, compare Scrooge's character with Cratchit's. What kind of men are they? Which man do you think is happier and more content? Why? In your response, cite details from the excerpt of Scene 2.

13. Young Ebenezer in Act I, Scene 5, of *A Christmas Carol: Scrooge and Marley* is very different from Scrooge of Act I, Scene 2. In an essay, contrast the younger Ebenezer with the older Scrooge. What differences do you see in their actions and in what they say? How is their treatment of other people different? Refer to at least one detail from each scene to support your points.

14. **Thinking About the Big Question: Do others see us more clearly than we see ourselves?** When Scrooge visits the past in Act I, Scene 5, of *A Christmas Carol: Scrooge and Marley*, he sees himself as a younger man. What does he realize about himself when he sees Young Ebenezer? In an essay, explain what Scrooge learns from his visit to Fezziwig's. How does the way he sees himself change as a result of the visit? Support your response with details from the scene.

Oral Response

15. Go back to question 2, 6, or 9 or to the question your teacher assigns you. Take a few minutes to expand your answer and prepare an oral response. Find additional details in Act I, Scenes 2 and 5, of *A Christmas Carol: Scrooge and Marley* that support your points. If necessary, make notes to guide your oral response.

from A Christmas Carol: Scrooge and Marley, *Act I, Scenes 2 & 5* by Israel Horovitz
Selection Test A

Critical Reading *Identify the letter of the choice that best answers the question.*

___ 1. In Act I, Scene 2, of *A Christmas Carol: Scrooge and Marley*, why is Bob Cratchit eager to go home?
  A. It is cold in the office.
  B. It is Christmas Eve.
  C. He does not like Scrooge.
  D. He fears he will be asked to work late.

___ 2. According to Act I, Scene 2, of *A Christmas Carol: Scrooge and Marley*, why does Scrooge dislike the idea of giving Cratchit a day off?
  A. Scrooge must pay him for the day.
  B. Cratchit does not work very hard.
  C. It is expected to be a busy day.
  D. Scrooge does not like Christmas.

___ 3. According to Act I, Scene 2, of *A Christmas Carol: Scrooge and Marley*, what is it that Cratchit tries to say to Scrooge that Scrooge does not want to hear?
  A. "I would like tomorrow off."
  B. "Have a good evening."
  C. "Christmas comes only once a year."
  D. "Merry Christmas."

___ 4. In Act I, Scene 2, of *A Christmas Carol: Scrooge and Marley*, why does Cratchit rush away after he says, "Merry Christmas, Mr. Scrooge"?
  A. He fears that Scrooge will ask him to work late.
  B. He knows that he has made Scrooge angry.
  C. He knows that Scrooge does not celebrate Christmas.
  D. He knows that Scrooge is also in a hurry to leave.

___ 5. Which word gives the best overall description of Scrooge in Act I, Scene 2, of *A Christmas Carol: Scrooge and Marley*?
  A. insincere
  B. greedy
  C. kind
  D. loud

_____ 6. According to Act I, Scene 5, of *A Christmas Carol: Scrooge and Marley*, what is the relationship between Fezziwig and young Scrooge?

  A. Fezziwig is Scrooge's uncle.

  B. Fezziwig is Scrooge's teacher.

  C. Fezziwig is Scrooge's master.

  D. Fezziwig is Scrooge's father.

_____ 7. In Act I, Scene 5, of *A Christmas Carol: Scrooge and Marley*, why does Fezziwig tell Dick Wilkins and Scrooge to stop working?

  A. He cannot pay their salary.

  B. He is going to scold them.

  C. It is the end of the day.

  D. It is Christmas Eve.

_____ 8. In the Christmas festivities that take place in Act I, Scene 5, of *A Christmas Carol: Scrooge and Marley*, whom does Fezziwig include?

  A. just his family

  B. just his employees

  C. just his friends

  D. everyone

_____ 9. According to Act I, Scene 5, of *A Christmas Carol: Scrooge and Marley*, how do Dick Wilkins and the young Scrooge feel about Mr. Fezziwig?

  A. They do not think about him.

  B. They dislike him.

  C. They think he is fair, but dull.

  D. They admire him.

_____ 10. Which word gives the best overall description of Fezziwig in Act I, Scene 5, of *A Christmas Carol: Scrooge and Marley*?

  A. generous

  B. businesslike

  C. sincere

  D. silly

_____ 11. Fezziwig, in Act I, Scene 5, of *A Christmas Carol: Scrooge and Marley*, is contrasted with Scrooge in Scene 2. In drama, what is the name for a character who is contrasted with another character to help develop that character?

  A. a main character

  B. a motivated character

  C. a foil

  D. an understudy

___ **12.** Which statement does *not* accurately describe Fezziwig and Scrooge?

    A. Fezziwig is poor; Scrooge is wealthy.

    B. Fezziwig has family; Scrooge is alone.

    C. Fezziwig is kind; Scrooge is harsh.

    D. Fezziwig is giving; Scrooge is selfish.

Vocabulary

___ **13.** Which is an instrument that a *fiddler* would play?

    A. a harp   **C.** a drum

    B. a guitar   **D.** a violin

___ **14.** Why are *suitors* following Fezziwig's daughters?

    A. They are interested in marrying them.

    B. They are the daughters' servants.

    C. They think the daughters are pretty.

    D. They are the daughters' tailors.

___ **15.** Which sentence uses the word *snuffs* correctly?

    A. The clerk <u>snuffs</u> the documents before presenting them to his boss.

    B. On the coldest days, we wear earmuffs, <u>snuffs</u>, and lined gloves.

    C. The waitress <u>snuffs</u> the candles at each table at the end of her shift.

    D. The baker proudly placed one dozen frosted <u>snuffs</u> in the box.

Essay

16. Ebenezer Scrooge employs one assistant. In an essay, describe Scrooge as a boss. How does he treat his employee? Is he fair? Is he understanding? Would you want to work for him? Why or why not? Cite two details from Act I, Scene 2, of *A Christmas Carol: Scrooge and Marley* to support your response.

17. Like Scrooge, Fezziwig owns a business. He has two apprentices, and he has a family. In an essay, tell more about Fezziwig. What is he like? How does he treat his employees? Is he fair? Is he understanding? What do others think of him? Would you want to work for someone like him? Why or why not? Cite two details from Act I, Scene 5, of *A Christmas Carol: Scrooge and Marley* to support your response.

18. Thinking About the Big Question: Do others see us more clearly than we see ourselves? When Scrooge visits the past in Act I, Scene 5, of *A Christmas Carol: Scrooge and Marley*, he sees himself as a younger man. In an essay, explain what Scrooge realizes about himself when he sees Young Ebenezer. Support your response with details from the scene.

from A Christmas Carol: Scrooge and Marley, *Act I, Scenes 2 & 5* by Israel Horovitz
Selection Test B

Critical Reading *Identify the letter of the choice that best completes the statement or answers the question.*

_____ 1. According to Act I, Scene 2, of *A Christmas Carol: Scrooge and Marley*, Scrooge resents having to give Bob Cratchit a day off for Christmas because
A. he knows that the firm will be busy on Christmas Day.
B. he dislikes being alone on Christmas Day.
C. he does not want to pay Cratchit for a day he does not work.
D. he had planned to fire Cratchit on Christmas Day.

_____ 2. In Act I, Scene 2, of *A Christmas Carol: Scrooge and Marley*, what does Scrooge suggest that Cratchit is doing by receiving a day's wages without working for it?
A. cheating him
B. mocking his business
C. picking his pocket
D. making excuses

_____ 3. According to Act I, Scene 2, of *A Christmas Carol: Scrooge and Marley*, why does Scrooge object when people enjoy Christmas?
A. He feels sad on Christmas because Marley died on Christmas Eve.
B. He cares only for making money, and Christmas interrupts business.
C. He believes that people should be kind and generous all year round.
D. He believes poor people should always be unhappy, even at Christmas.

_____ 4. In Act I, Scene 2, of *A Christmas Carol: Scrooge and Marley*, why does Cratchit wait until he is ready to leave to wish Scrooge a merry Christmas?
A. Cratchit knows that Scrooge will be insulted if he does not say it.
B. Cratchit is afraid that Scrooge will fire him for saying it.
C. Cratchit is afraid that Scrooge might throw something at him.
D. Cratchit knows that Scrooge does not want him to mention Christmas.

_____ 5. Which word best describes Scrooge's motivation in Act I, Scene 2, of *A Christmas Carol: Scrooge and Marley*?
A. hatred
B. pain
C. greed
D. happiness

_____ 6. According to Act I, Scene 5, of *A Christmas Carol: Scrooge and Marley*, what is the relationship between Scrooge and Fezziwig?
A. Scrooge is Fezziwig's servant.
B. Scrooge is Fezziwig's nephew.
C. Scrooge is Fezziwig's student.
D. Scrooge is Fezziwig's apprentice.

____ **7.** According to Act I, Scene 5, of *A Christmas Carol: Scrooge and Marley*, what is the relationship between Scrooge and Dick Wilkins?
    A. Wilkins is Scrooge's employer.
    B. Scrooge is Wilkins's employer.
    C. Scrooge and Wilkins are partners.
    D. Wilkins and Scrooge are apprentices.

____ **8.** According to Act I, Scene 5, of *A Christmas Carol: Scrooge and Marley*, who was kind to Scrooge in his past?
    I. Fezziwig
    II. the fiddler
    III. Fezziwig's daughters
    IV. Dick Wilkins
    A. I, II, III   C. I, II, IV
    B. I, III, IV   D. II, III, IV

____ **9.** According to Act I, Scene 5, of *A Christmas Carol: Scrooge and Marley*, Fezziwig's Christmas festivities include
    A. only Fezziwig's family.
    B. only Fezziwig's employees.
    C. only Fezziwig's daughters' suitors.
    D. Fezziwig's family, his employees, and his daughters' suitors.

____ **10.** According to Act I, Scene 5, of *A Christmas Carol: Scrooge and Marley*, what does young Scrooge feel toward Fezziwig?
    A. gratitude   C. dignity
    B. love   D. disrespect

____ **11.** What is ironic about this statement by young Scrooge in Act I, Scene 5, of *A Christmas Carol: Scrooge and Marley*?
    If ever I own a firm of my own, I shall treat my apprentices with the same dignity and the same grace.
    A. Although young Scrooge thinks his master is nice, the man treats others unkindly.
    B. After young Scrooge says this, his master mistreats him and fires him.
    C. Scrooge remains an apprentice all his life and is never again treated so well.
    D. When Scrooge does have his own firm, he treats his employee harshly.

____ **12.** Which adjectives best describe Fezziwig?
    A. silly and happy   C. jolly and fat
    B. kind and intelligent   D. kind and generous

____ **13.** How does Fezziwig's treatment of others in Act I, Scene 5, of *A Christmas Carol: Scrooge and Marley* contrast with Scrooge's treatment of others in Scene 2?
    A. Fezziwig is generous to everyone, while Scrooge is cold and harsh to everyone.
    B. Fezziwig is not serious about work, while Scrooge is dedicated to his business.
    C. Fezziwig is foolish and silly, while Scrooge is intelligent and serious.
    D. Fezziwig treats his wife and children well, while Scrooge neglects his family.

___ 14. How does Fezziwig, in Act I, Scene 5, of *A Christmas Carol: Scrooge and Marley*, fulfill the role of a *foil*?
   A. He reinforces the theme of the play.
   B. He serves as a contrast to Scrooge.
   C. He adds comic relief to the play.
   D. He frustrates Scrooge's ambitions.

Vocabulary

___ 15. In Act I, Scene 5, of *A Christmas Carol: Scrooge and Marley*, whom can the reader assume the *suitors* have come to see?
   A. Fezziwig
   B. Fezziwig's daughters
   C. Fezziwig's wife
   D. Scrooge and Wilkins

___ 16. Before leaving for the evening, Cratchit *snuffs* out
   A. a document.
   B. a candle.
   C. the clock.
   D. the lights.

___ 17. In which sentence is the word *fiddler* used correctly?
   A. The *fiddler* in the country band played his violin energetically.
   B. The *fiddler* in the service station tuned up the engine perfectly.
   C. The *fiddler* in the orchestra tuned all of the stringed instruments.
   D. The *fiddler* in the accounting department audited the firm's records.

Essay

18. The brief dialogue between Scrooge and Cratchit in Act I, Scene 2, of *A Christmas Carol: Scrooge and Marley* gives the audience a great deal of insight into Scrooge's character. In an essay, compare Scrooge's character with Cratchit's. Answer these questions: What kind of man is Scrooge? How does he treat his employee? What kind of man is Bob Cratchit? How does he treat his employer? Which man would make a better boss? Why? In your response, cite at least two details from the excerpt of Scene 2.

19. Young Ebenezer Scrooge, in Act I, Scene 5, of *A Christmas Carol: Scrooge and Marley*, is very different from the Ebenezer Scrooge of Scene 2. In an essay, contrast the young Scrooge and the older Scrooge. What differences do you see in their actions? What differences do you see in what they say? What differences do you see in how they treat other people? Refer to at least one detail from each scene to support your points.

20. **Thinking About the Big Question: Do others see us more clearly than we see ourselves?** When Scrooge visits the past in Act I, Scene 5, of *A Christmas Carol: Scrooge and Marley*, he sees himself as a younger man. What does he realize about himself when he sees Young Ebenezer? In an essay, explain what Scrooge learns from his visit to Fezziwig's. How does the way he sees himself change as a result of the visit. Support your response with details from the scene.

Unit 5 Resources: Drama
81

Name _____ Date _____

Research: Multimedia Report

Prewriting: Gathering Details

Answer the questions in the chart below to help you choose your visual and audio sources.

Questions	Your Answers
What is your presentation about?	
Who is your audience?	
What is your purpose?	
What audio sources could you creatively use in your presentation?	
What video sources could you creatively use in your presentation?	

Drafting: Providing Elaboration

Use the following graphic organizer to help you decide how to use audio and visual aids to enhance your presentation.

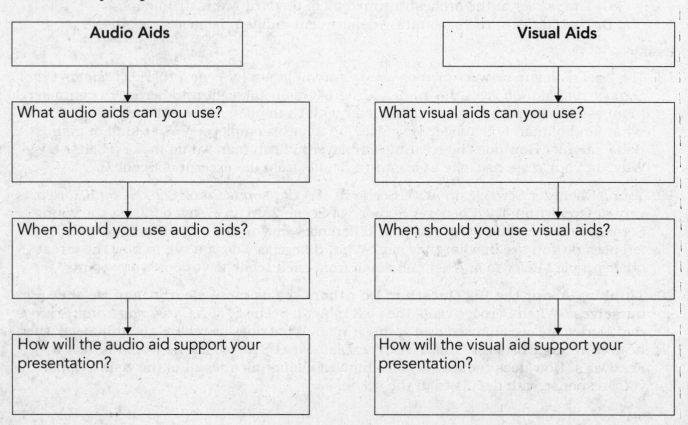

Audio Aids	Visual Aids
What audio aids can you use?	What visual aids can you use?
When should you use audio aids?	When should you use visual aids?
How will the audio aid support your presentation?	How will the visual aid support your presentation?

Writing Workshop—Unit 5, Part 1
Multimedia Report: Integrating Grammar Skills

Revising to Avoid Common Usage Problems

Be careful to use the following words correctly in your writing.

Word	Meaning	Example
Accept	verb, "to agree to" or "to take what is offered"	Everyone *except* Jo will *accept* what I have to say.
Except	preposition, "leaving out" or "other than"	
Affect	verb, "to influence" or "to cause a change in"	Too much sun can *affect* your eyes, although the *effect* is usually temporary.
Effect	usually a noun, means "a result"	
Advice	noun, "an opinion"	I listen to good *advice* and *advise* others as best I can.
Advise	verb, "to give an opinion"	
Beside	preposition, "at the side of" or "close to"	Did anyone *besides* Jon sit *beside* the waterfall?
Besides	preposition, "in addition to" or "other than"	
In	preposition, refers to position	I went *into* the car and then sat *in* traffic for hours.
Into	preposition, suggests motion	

Identifying Correct Usage

A. DIRECTIONS: *Complete each sentence by circling the correct choice in parentheses.*

1. I sat (beside, besides) Sandy at the basketball game after school.
2. Everyone (accept, except) Sharon went to the game.
3. Sharon went (in, into) the guidance counselor's office.
4. The counselor offered her good (advice, advise) about schoolwork.
5. Following the suggestions may have an (affect, effect) on Sharon's grades.

Fixing Common Usage Problems

B. DIRECTIONS: *On the lines provided, rewrite these sentences so that they use the correct words. If a sentence is correct as presented, write* correct.

1. Did anyone except Lola accept the invitation?

_____

2. I would advice you to go in the house before it rains.

_____

3. Many people besides me except my mother's advise.

_____

Unit 5: Drama
Benchmark Test 9

MULTIPLE CHOICE

Reading Skill: Purpose for Reading *Read the selection. Then, answer the questions that follow.*

Thinking Big: The Man Who Changed Our View of the Universe

At the age of 30, Edwin Hubble—the "Hubble" of the Hubble Space Telescope, which gives us views of distant galaxies—was intrigued by the stars and the possibility of worlds beyond our own. In 1919, Hubble left his successful law practice and returned to the study of astronomy. Just a few years later, Hubble made some of the most important discoveries of all time. He found that there were galaxies beyond the Milky Way and discovered that the universe is continually expanding. Although Hubble died more than fifty years ago, scientists today are still "expanding" on Hubble's momentous discoveries.

1. What does the title of the selection suggest?
   A. The selection is a work of fiction.
   B. The selection is about important discoveries.
   C. The selection was written by a student.
   D. The selection is from an Internet Web site.

2. Based on the title and first sentence, which of the following best states a purpose for reading the selection?
   A. to learn about an important scientist
   B. to learn about the practice of law
   C. to be entertained by an amusing story
   D. to analyze a theory about the universe

3. Why is it important to preview the selection after setting a purpose for reading?
   A. to help you outline the main ideas and details
   B. to help you set more than one purpose for reading
   C. to help you identify unfamiliar words in the text
   D. to help you decide if the selection will fit your purpose

4. Which of the following might best help you preview a literary work before reading it?
   A. the order in which events occur
   B. the author's biography
   C. the point of view of the narrator
   D. the way the text is organized

Read the selection. Then, answer the questions that follow.

Using the Memory Function of Your Cell Phone

Let's face it: you're on the go. And you've got a lot on your mind. You can't be expected to remember all the important phone numbers you need to know. Let your phone remember them for you. Here's how to use the phone memory feature:

1. Enter the phone number you want to store.
2. Press *STO* to begin storing. You will see: *Location XX?*
3. Press *STO* again to store the sequence in the displayed location.

4. Enter a digit and press the star key to store the sequence in the first available location beginning with that digit.

5. Scroll through the icons and press *STO* to select a highlighted icon.

5. Why might you read the introduction more quickly than the directions in this selection?
   A. The introduction is more important to understanding the task.
   B. The introduction is written at a simpler level.
   C. The introduction is more promotional than useful.
   D. The introduction is written as a paragraph.

6. Which of the following is best read slowly?
   A. a recipe with many steps
   B. an advertisement for toothpaste
   C. a comic strip
   D. an exciting short story

7. Which of the following influences your reading rate?
   A. the author's purpose
   B. your purpose for reading
   C. the length of the text
   D. the author's skill as a writer

Reading Skill: Analyze the Author's Perspective

Read the selection. Then, answer the questions that follow.

Think you've read *Charlotte's Web*? Read it again. You'll find this American classic to be full of surprises you missed during your first reading. As almost everyone knows, the book by E. B. White is the story of a girl who befriends a runt of a pig named Wilbur. The girl saves Wilbur's life, which is again saved, later in the story, by a remarkable spider named Charlotte. *Charlotte's Web* is an elegantly written fantasy with moral overtones and gentle wisdom about life and death.

8. What is one purpose for reading literary criticism, such as this selection?
   A. to decide whether to read a work
   B. to analyze a literary work
   C. to learn about a book's author
   D. to judge a literary work

9. Which phrase from the selection best illustrates the critic's opinion of *Charlotte's Web*?
   A. elegantly written fantasy
   B. American classic
   C. remarkable spider
   D. gentle wisdom

10. Which of the following best describes the critic's feelings about *Charlotte's Web*?
    A. The critic thinks the book is charming.
    B. The critic admires E. B. White.
    C. The critic recommends the book.
    D. The critic strongly likes the book.

Literary Analysis: Dialogue *Read the selection. Then, answer the questions that follow.*

Brendan joined his brother outside the school. "I lost the election," he told Sam.

"What?!" Sam exclaimed, and then narrowed his eyes. "You are the world's *greatest* pessimist," he said. "Have they counted all the votes?"

Brendan shrugged and glanced woefully to the side, "Well—no. But I just came from the gym and I could just *feel* that the votes weren't going my way."

"Come on, buddy," Sam said, heading back into the school. "We're going to stay until we know for sure whether or not you won. I don't want to spend an evening with you moaning about losing—especially if you won."

11. Which of the following best describes dialogue in a literary work?
    A. a conversation between characters
    B. a portrait of a character
    C. a way a writer reveals the plot
    D. a struggle between opposing forces

12. What does the dialogue in the selection reveal about Sam?
    A. He is older than Brendan.
    B. He is supportive of Brendan.
    C. He often disagrees with Brendan.
    D. He is jealous of Brendan.

13. Why is the last line "Come on, buddy" significant?
    A. It shows that Sam is impatient.
    B. It shows that Sam is playful.
    C. It shows Sam's affection for Brendan.
    D. It shows Sam's teasing nature.

Literary Analysis: Stage Directions *Read the stage directions below. Then, answer the questions that follow.*

[*It is early morning in the Vargas house. Kyle's parents and his sister are still asleep. The faint light of dawn can be seen through the window of Kyle's bedroom, where he stands in front of a full-length mirror. In the distance can be heard the sound of a chirping bird. Kyle holds several note cards in his hand. He studies one of the cards for a minute. Then he squares his shoulders, looks confidently into the mirror, and recites the opening line of his speech.*]

14. What are stage directions in a dramatic script?
    A. the way in which events unfold
    B. the words not spoken by characters
    C. the central message in a play
    D. conversations among characters

15. What information about the setting is included in the stage directions of the selection?
    A. the type of speech Kyle will give
    B. the first line of Kyle's speech
    C. a description of the lighting
    D. the theme of the play

16. To whom might these stage directions be most useful?
    A. to someone who is reading the play
    B. to someone who is reviewing the play
    C. to someone who is watching the play
    D. to the author of the play

Name _____ Date _____

Literary Analysis: Comparing Characters *Read the excerpt from a dramatic script. Then, answer the questions that follow.*

ANNE. [*She studies a receipt.*] The clerk forgot to charge me for one of these books.

JOANIE. Great! You got a free book, then.

ANNE. What? Are you saying that I shouldn't go back and tell him?

JOANIE. Don't be silly. The store probably won't notice, so just consider it a little gift. Besides, that store charges too much for books.

ANNE. I'd feel terrible. I couldn't enjoy the book for thinking about not paying for it. It's just not right.

JOANIE. [*Shaking her head.*] Suit yourself. But I think you're being too righteous about the whole thing.

17. Which of the following best describes Anne?
    A. careful
    B. confused
    C. silly
    D. honest

18. Based on the selection, which of the following is probably true of Joanie?
    A. She is uncomfortable around Anne.
    B. She has a strong sense of fairness.
    C. She can justify being dishonest.
    D. She is easily influenced by Anne.

19. How are Anne and Joanie different?
    A. Anne is more concerned than Joanie about what others think.
    B. Anne is more influenced by her conscience than is Joanie.
    C. Joanie thinks things through more carefully than does Anne.
    D. Joanie is more easily upset than is Anne.

Vocabulary: Roots and Prefixes

20. What does the root *-grat-* mean in the word *gratification*?
    A. free
    B. pleasing
    C. angry
    D. helpful

21. Based on your knowledge of the root *-grat-*, when would a person show *gratitude*?
    A. after being scared
    B. after being fired
    C. after receiving a raise
    D. after an argument

22. Using your knowledge of the root *-grat-*, what does the word *ingrate* mean in the following sentence?

    John was such an ingrate that he did not say anything to a friend who had helped him repair his car.

    A. an ungrateful person
    B. a friendly person
    C. an interesting person
    D. a quiet person

23. Using your knowledge of the prefix *inter-*, what does the word *intermingled* mean in the following sentence?

The grapefruits and oranges became intermingled after falling onto the floor.

A. worthless

B. contaminated

C. mixed together

D. damaged

24. Based on your knowledge of the prefix *inter-*, when would a musical *interlude* occur?

A. at the very end of a song

B. in the middle of a song

C. in place of a song

D. before the song

25. Based on your knowledge of the prefix *inter-*, what is an *interface*?

A. an instruction

B. a body part

C. a connection

D. a solution

Grammar: Using Interjections

26. Which of the following best describes an interjection?

A. a word used to join groups of words

B. a noun that identifies another noun

C. a part of speech that expresses emotion

D. a part of speech that modifies a verb

27. Which of the following sentences contains an interjection?

A. Where did you put the box of clothes?

B. The actor groaned miserably.

C. All of the coins are missing!

D. Oops, I think I pressed the wrong key.

28. Which word in the following sentence is an interjection?

Wow, aren't computers amazing?

A. Wow

B. aren't

C. computers

D. amazing

Grammar: Double Negatives

29. Which of the following words is a negative word?

Alejandro remarked bitterly that they were going nowhere slowly.

A. remarked

B. bitterly

C. nowhere

D. slowly

30. What is the best way to correct the double negative in the following sentence?

I never see no one I know at the park.

A. I never see anyone I know at the park.

B. I do not ever see nobody I know at the park.

C. I never do not see anyone I know at the park.

D. I do not see no one I know at the park.

31. Which of the following sentences contains a double negative?
    A. Tanya will not go near the ocean.
    B. Mr. Fell had nothing bad to say.
    C. I never listen to anyone who gossips.
    D. We do not have no extra tables.

Grammar: Revising to Avoid Common Usage Problems

32. What is the meaning of *affect* in the following sentence?

    The wet weather did not affect Josh's performance in the bike race.

    A. bring about
    B. influence
    C. result in
    D. cause

33. In which sentence is *accept* used correctly?
    A. Trenell made all A's accept in science.
    B. Everyone accept Bonnie was there.
    C. I like all vegetables accept beets.
    D. Will the writer accept both awards?

ESSAY

Writing

34. Suppose that your school is considering adding tap dancing as a PE course. Write a brief letter to your principal giving your opinion about the decision. State at least two reasons and provide supporting details. Remember to include a salutation and your signature in your letter. Remember to state a firm point of view.

35. Think of a friend, family member, or neighbor who has qualities that you admire. Write a brief tribute, or expression of admiration, to this person. Your tribute can include a story of a time when this person particularly influenced you, or write about two or three qualities that you most admire in this person. Write a concluding statement at the end of your tribute.

36. Write a paragraph that describes a plan for a multimedia report. In your plan, tell about the topic of the report and describe how the report will be organized. Describe the media—print and nonprint—that you plan to use and tell about the effect you hope to create in the report.

Name _____

Unit 5: Drama Skills Concept Map—2

Do others see us more clearly than we see ourselves?

Literary Analysis:
Drama

Reading Skills and Strategies:
Summaries

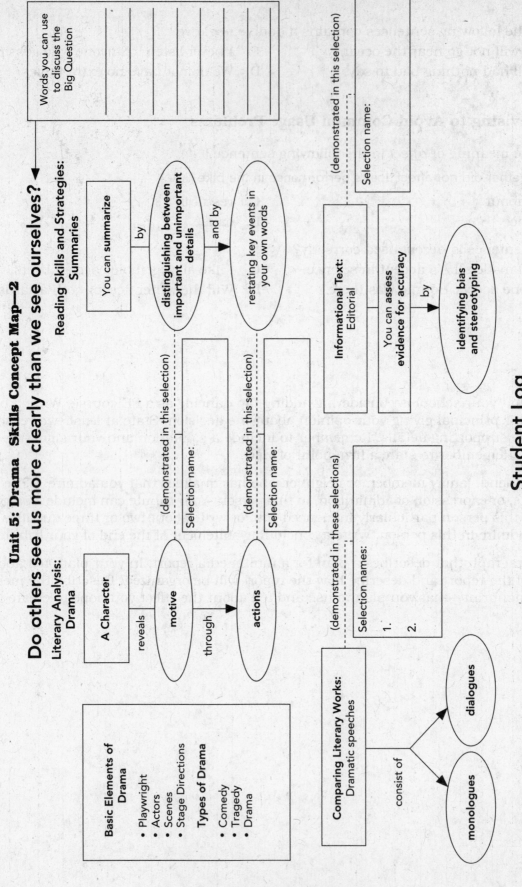

Basic Elements of Drama

- Playwright
- Actors
- Scenes
- Stage Directions

Types of Drama

- Comedy
- Tragedy
- Drama

A Character — reveals → motive — through → actions

You can summarize — by → distinguishing between important and unimportant details — and by → restating key events in your own words

(demonstrated in this selection)
Selection name:

(demonstrated in this selection)
Selection name:

Informational Text:
Editorial

You can assess evidence for accuracy — by → identifying bias and stereotyping

(demonstrated in this selection)
Selection name:

Comparing Literary Works:
Dramatic speeches — consist of → dialogues / monologues

(demonstrated in these selections)
Selection names:
1.
2.

Student Log

Complete this chart to track your assignments.

Writing	Extend Your Learning	Writing Workshop	Other Assignments

Words you can use to discuss the Big Question

Vocabulary Warm-up Word Lists

Study these words from "The Monsters Are Due on Maple Street." Then, complete the activities that follow.

Word List A

afford [uh FAWRD] *v.* to have enough money to buy something
   Susan made enough money to <u>afford</u> a new car.

broadcast [BRAWD kast] *n.* television or radio program
   I was in school when the first news <u>broadcast</u> about the attack on the Pentagon aired.

gradually [GRAJ oo uhl lee] *adv.* slowly but steadily
   To make a good soufflé, combine the ingredients <u>gradually</u>.

hesitant [HEZ i tuhnt] *adj.* unwilling to do something because you are unsure or worried
   Pat was <u>hesitant</u> to ask her parents for a new cell phone.

mildly [MYLD lee] *adv.* slightly
   We were only <u>mildly</u> interested in the senator's speech.

obviously [AHB vee uhs lee] *adv.* easily seen or understood
   The photographer was <u>obviously</u> more interested in nature than in cityscapes.

process [PROS es] *n.* series of actions or changes to achieve a particular result
   Jerry is in the <u>process</u> of rebuilding his glider.

typical [TIP i kuhl] *adj.* having the qualities of a particular thing, person, or group
   At age 2, the <u>typical</u> child talks in two-word sentences.

Word List B

dimension [di MEN shuhn] *n.* level of consciousness, existence, or reality
   We can go beyond ordinary time and space through the <u>dimension</u> of our imaginations.

intense [in TENS] *adj.* serious and having very strong feelings
   The president gave an <u>intense</u> speech on the problem of world hunger.

prejudices [prej uh dis ez] *n.* opinions formed hastily without careful thought
   People's <u>prejudices</u> are often based on fear or misinformation.

reaction [ree AK shuhn] *n.* action or feeling in response to something
   The public <u>reaction</u> to the mayor's decision to resign was complete surprise.

reflective [ri FLEK tiv] *adj.* serious and thoughtful
   After watching the movie, James left the theater in a <u>reflective</u> mood.

residential [rez i DEN shuhl] *adj.* having to do with private homes
   We moved from the city to a quiet <u>residential</u> neighborhood.

tremendous [tri MEN duhs] *adj.* huge; enormous
   The audience gave the orchestra a <u>tremendous</u> ovation.

unique [yoo NEEK] *adj.* one of a kind; unlike anything else
   Because every set of fingerprints is <u>unique</u>, it is often used as a means of identification.

"The Monsters Are Due on Maple Street" by Rod Serling
Vocabulary Warm-up Exercises

Exercise A *Fill in each blank in the paragraph below with an appropriate word from Word List A. Use each word only once.*

Marcie couldn't [1]_____ to buy one of those hand-held music play-

ers, so she listened to a music [2] _____ on her portable radio. At first

she was [3] _____ to admit to her friends that she listened to the radio,

but one day that changed. While Marcie was in the [4]_____ of adjusting

the radio tuner, she came across a public radio station. She listened for a while and

discovered that the programs were not [5] _____ of other stations.

[6] _____, she tuned into this station more and more. She enjoyed the

lively conversations about world events. When she told her friends, they were only

[7] _____ interested. [8] _____, her friends wanted to

listen only to music. Marcie felt they were missing something special.

Exercise B *Circle T if the statement is true or F if the statement is false. Then, explain your answer.*

1. Reaching the top of Mount Everest is a <u>tremendous</u> accomplishment.
   T / F _____

2. A <u>residential</u> area is a great place to go camping.
   T / F _____

3. If you lose something <u>unique</u> you can always get another one.
   T / F _____

4. It is always fun to be with a person who is very <u>intense</u>.
   T / F _____

5. It is natural to be <u>reflective</u> when you are in a hurry.
   T / F _____

6. Dreams occur in another <u>dimension</u>.
   T / F _____

7. One typical audience <u>reaction</u> to a good horror movie is lots of screaming.
   T / F _____

8. A person can never overcome his or her <u>prejudices</u>.
   T / F _____

"The Monsters Are Due on Maple Street" by Rod Serling

Reading Warm-up A

Read the following passage. Pay special attention to the underlined words. Then, read it again, and complete the activities. Use a separate sheet of paper for your written answers.

If you had a time machine in your home, would you use it? Chances are you would. Maybe you already do, for there really is a time machine in your home. It's tucked inside your TV. Today you can turn on the cable channels that rerun old television shows and witness life in America as far back as 1950.

Before 1950, home televisions had been around for about three years, but most people couldn't <u>afford</u> them. The <u>typical</u> set was a big wooden box with a tiny 10-inch or 15-inch video screen. The picture was black and white and fuzzy. TVs were expensive because they were new and excitingly different. Unfortunately, the shows were only <u>mildly</u> entertaining. One popular show was wrestling. The viewers were wild about a wrestler named Gorgeous George. He wore hairpins in his hair.

<u>Gradually</u>, the screens got bigger. The picture improved, and so did the shows. By the early 1950s, stations offered several kinds of programs: plays, newscasts, old movies, variety and talent shows. A favorite <u>broadcast</u> of the '50s was the situation comedy, or "sitcom." Sitcoms, such as *I Love Lucy*, found the humor in everyday life.

Commercials were really big, too, even then. By 1954, television manufacturers were in the <u>process</u> of discontinuing black-and-white TVs and introducing color. People were no longer <u>hesitant</u> to buy a TV set. Everybody was eager to have one.

It was during the '50s that families started eating prepackaged dinners while watching their favorite TV shows. Americans also began to believe that the families shown on *Leave It to Beaver* and *Father Knows Best* represented the normal American family—so what was wrong with *their* families? <u>Obviously</u>, early TV often presented an unreal picture of real America. Still, much that was on TV then was just as real as it is today. Keep that in mind the next time you watch a rerun, grab a TV dinner, and travel back to the '50s.

1. Circle the word that tells what people couldn't <u>afford</u>. Write the meaning of *afford*.

2. Underline the words that describe a <u>typical</u> TV set of the '50s. Describe a *typical* TV set of today.

3. Circle the word described as only <u>mildly</u> entertaining. Rewrite the sentence using a synonym for *mildly*.

4. Underline the words that tell what happened <u>gradually</u>. Write about something else that happens *gradually*.

5. Underline the words that name a favorite <u>broadcast</u> of the '50s. Write about your favorite kind of *broadcast*.

6. Underline the words that tell what manufacturers were in the <u>process</u> of doing by 1954. Write about something you are in the *process* of doing.

7. Circle the word that means the opposite of <u>hesitant</u>. Write the meaning of *hesitant*.

8. Underline the words that tell what early TV <u>obviously</u> presented. Use a synonym for *obviously* in a sentence about TV.

"The Monsters Are Due on Maple Street" by Rod Serling
Reading Warm-up B

Read the following passage. Pay special attention to the underlined words. Then, read it again, and complete the activities. Use a separate sheet of paper for your written answers.

On October 2, 1959, the first episode of a science-fiction/fantasy show appeared on television. It was a "little show," only 30 minutes long, and in black and white, but it lit up the TV screen like nothing before. Perhaps you have heard of it. It was called *The Twilight Zone.*

In all of television, *The Twilight Zone* was <u>unique</u>; there was no other show like it at the time. Viewers didn't just watch it—they entered it. Each week they would find themselves in another small town, on a <u>residential</u> street lined with modest houses, or in a building that looked familiar, but not quite. They entered a <u>dimension</u> between dreams and imagination, but it felt like home. They left it feeling thoughtful and <u>reflective</u>.

Before each episode, Rod Serling, the writer and creator of the series, delivered a short but <u>intense</u> introduction.

NARRATOR'S VOICE. *Maple Street. Six-forty-four p.m. on a late September evening. [A pause] Maple Street in the last calm and reflective moment . . . before the monsters came!*

Although it was considered science fiction, *The Twilight Zone* was unlike later sci-fi shows that were set in another time and place. Many of the stories did take place in a not-too-distant future, and alien monsters occasionally would make an appearance. However, it was the monster within the human heart that most interested Rod Serling. His scripts explored political and social issues, <u>prejudices</u> against ideas and other people, injustice, and other human failings. His shows were a <u>tremendous</u> departure from other TV shows of the time, which were usually predictable and never political. Viewer <u>reaction</u> to *The Twilight Zone* proved that audiences were ready for more thoughtful programs.

The show still has loyal fans, not only because the stories are timeless, but also because, as Rod Serling would be the first to tell you, "At one time or another, we all live in *The Twilight Zone.*"

1. Underline the words that give the meaning of <u>unique</u>. Write a sentence using the word *unique.*

2. Underline the words that describe a <u>residential</u> street. Describe a *residential* street in your area.

3. Underline the words that describe the <u>dimension</u> viewers entered. Rewrite the sentence using a synonym for *dimension.*

4. Circle the word that means the same as <u>reflective</u>. Write a sentence using the word *reflective.*

5. Circle the word that tells what was short but <u>intense</u>. Describe a person you know or have read about who is *intense.*

6. Underline the words that tell what <u>prejudices</u> are against. Use *prejudices* in a sentence.

7. Circle the words that tell what was a <u>tremendous</u> departure. Underline the words that tell what they were a *tremendous* departure from. Give a synonym for *tremendous.*

8. Underline the words that tell what viewer <u>reaction</u> proved. Write the meaning of *reaction.*

Name _____ Date _____

Writing About the Big Question

Do others see us more clearly than we see ourselves?

Big Question Vocabulary

appearance	appreciate	assumption	bias	characteristic
define	focus	identify	ignore	image
perception	perspective	reaction	reflect	reveal

A. *Choose one word from the list above to complete each sentence. There may be more than one right answer.*

1. Most people have one _____ that is more notice-able than the others.

2. Sometimes it is hard to _____ your talents.

3. It is dangerous to _____ your shortcomings.

B. *Follow the directions in responding to each of the items below.*

1. List at least four ways that kids project an image to others.

   _____

   _____

2. Do you think school uniforms are a good idea? Write three or more sentences explaining your position. Use at least two of the Big Question vocabulary words. You may use the words in different forms (for example you can change *reflect* to *reflection*).

   _____

   _____

C. *Complete the sentence below. Then, write a short paragraph in which you connect this sentence to the big question.*

When gripped by fear, our reactions can sometimes _____

   _____

   _____

Name _____ Date _____

"The Monsters Are Due on Maple Street" by Rod Serling
Reading: Distinguish Between Important and Unimportant Details to Write a Summary

A **summary** is a brief statement that presents only the main ideas and most important details. Summarizing helps you review and understand what you are reading. To summarize, you must first **distinguish between important and unimportant details.** Ask yourself questions like these:

• Is the detail necessary to an understanding of the literary work?
• Would the work hold together without the inclusion of this information?

As you read, pause periodically to recall and restate only the key events and important details.

DIRECTIONS: *Read these summaries of portions of "The Monsters Are Due on Maple Street." Then, answer the questions that follow each summary.*

It is an ordinary September evening on Maple Street when a roar is heard and a flash is seen. The power goes off, and telephones and portable radios stop working. One neighbor leaves to see what is happening on another street. Another neighbor says that he will go downtown to find out what is going on. For no explainable reason, his car will not start. He and a third neighbor decide to walk downtown. Tommy, a fourteen-year-old boy who wears eyeglasses, tells the men not to go. Tommy tells the crowd that what is happening is like every story about aliens he has read. He says that before they land, aliens send a family that looks human to live in a community and prepare for the aliens' arrival.

1. What is the main idea of the preceding summary?

   _____

2. Which detail in the preceding summary is unnecessary?

   _____

After Les Goodman's car starts on its own, the neighbors become suspicious of Goodman. A neighbor says that she has seen him standing on his porch in the middle of the night, looking at the sky. Goodman explains that he often has insomnia. He compares his neighbors to frightened rabbits. He says that they are letting a nightmare begin.

3. What is the main idea of the preceding summary?

   _____

   _____

4. Which detail in the preceding summary is unimportant? How do you know it is unimportant?

   _____

   _____

Name _____ Date _____

"The Monsters Are Due on Maple Street" by Rod Serling
Literary Analysis: A Character's Motives

A character's motives are the reasons for his or her actions. Motives are usually related to what a character wants, needs, or feels. Powerful motives include love, anger, fear, and greed. As you read, think about what motivates each character.

DIRECTIONS: *Read the following passages from "The Monsters Are Due on Maple Street." Then, answer the questions that follow, about the characters' motives.*

STEVE. It isn't just the power failure, Charlie. If it was, we'd still be able to get a broadcast on the portable.

[*There's a murmur of reaction to this.* STEVE *looks from face to face and then over to his car.*]

STEVE. I'll run downtown. We'll get this all straightened out.

1. What are Steve's motives for volunteering to go downtown?

_____

_____

GOODMAN. I just don't understand it. I tried to start it and it wouldn't start. You saw me. All of you saw me.

[*And now, just as suddenly as the engine started, it stops and there's a long silence that is gradually intruded upon by the frightened murmuring of the people.*]

GOODMAN. I don't understand. I swear . . . I don't understand. What's happening?

DON. Maybe you better tell us. Nothing's working on this street. Nothing. No lights, no power, no radio. . . . Nothing except one car—yours!

[*The people pick this up and now their murmuring becomes a loud chant filling the air with accusations and demands for action. Two of the men . . . head toward* GOODMAN, *who backs away, backing into his car and now at bay.*]

GOODMAN. Wait a minute now. You keep your distance—all of you. So I've got a car that starts by itself—well, that's a freak thing. I admit it. But does that make me some kind of a criminal or something? I don't know why the car works—it just does!

2. Which speaker appears to be motivated by confusion? _____

3. Which speaker appears to be motivated by suspicion? _____

4. What emotion or emotions appear to be motivating Goodman after the crowd has accused him? _____

5. Why might Goodman be feeling this emotion? _____

_____

Name _____ Date _____

"The Monsters Are Due on Maple Street" by Rod Serling
Vocabulary Builder

Word List

defiant   flustered   metamorphosis   persistently   sluggishly   transfixed

A. DIRECTIONS: *Read each sentence, and think about the meaning of the italicized word from the Word List. Then, answer the question, and explain your answer.*

1. Would you expect a *flustered* person to speak clearly?

   _____

2. If a heavy rain fills a riverbed, will the river move *sluggishly*?

   _____

3. If someone *persistently* asks a question, would you assume that she is eager to know the answer?

   _____

4. Would a *defiant* child be likely to refuse to do his chores?

   _____

5. If a rude person undergoes a *metamorphosis*, is she likely to continue to be rude?

   _____

6. If a person is *transfixed* by a performance, does he find it interesting?

   _____

B. WORD STUDY: *The Latin root -sist- means "stand." Read the following sentences. Use your knowledge of the root -sist- to write a full sentence to answer each question. Include the italicized word in your answer.*

1. Is an *assistant* someone who competes with you?

   _____

2. If you *insist* on doing something, are you expressing yourself in a firm manner?

   _____

3. Is a *persistent* person going to give up easily?

   _____

"The Monsters Are Due on Maple Street" by Rod Serling
Enrichment: Script Writing

If any character in "The Monsters Are Due on Maple Street" reflects Rod Serling's philosophy, it is Steve Brand. Throughout the play, Steve tries to persuade his neighbors to choose reason and common sense over suspicion and violence.

DIRECTIONS: *Prepare to write a script for a half-hour science-fiction television series—a modern-day* Twilight Zone. *Like Serling, you will require ordinary people to face an extraordinary situation. And like Serling's work, your screenplay will teach a lesson as well as entertain. Gather your ideas by responding to the following prompts. (Read all the prompts before you begin writing. You may not want to respond in order.)*

Setting: When and where will the events take place? Will your screenplay be set in the present, in the past, or in the future? Will it take place on this planet, on another planet, or in a spacecraft? _____

_____

Characters: Will your characters be humans or aliens, or will the two interact? Think about your characters' beliefs, their education and family background, their occupation (Are they adults who hold jobs? Are they students?), their talents, their fears, their quirks. Describe two or three main characters, including the most important details.

_____

_____

Plot: Here is where you have to figure out—and describe—what happens to your characters. The events should be very unusual, and they should create a problem for the characters to resolve. Briefly describe the plot, including the conflict and the resolution.

_____

_____

_____

Message: What lesson will your screenplay teach? Which character will convey the message? At what point will he or she do it?

_____

_____

Now, write the dialogue for one brief scene in your screenplay.

_____

_____

_____

_____

_____

_____

"The Monsters Are Due on Maple Street" by Rod Serling
Integrated Language Skills: Grammar

Sentence Functions and Endmarks

Sentences are classified into four categories, according to their function.

Category, Function, and Endmark	Example
A **declarative sentence** makes a statement. It ends with a period. (.)	Monsters are due on Maple Street.
An **interrogative sentence** asks a question. It ends with a question mark. (?)	What is going on?
An **imperative sentence** gives a command. It ends with a period or an exclamation point. (. or !)	Do not leave town. Watch out!
An **exclamatory sentence** calls out or exclaims. It ends with an exclamation point. (!)	Hey! How frightened we were!

Note that the subject of an imperative sentence is always the word *you*, and it is never stated: *(You) do not leave town. (You) watch out!*

Also note that in your writing, you should use exclamatory sentences as if they were a powerful spice. For the greatest effect, use them sparingly.

A. DIRECTIONS: *Add the correct endmark to each sentence. Then, identify the sentence as* declarative, interrogative, imperative, *or* exclamatory.

1. Where did you go on your field trip on Saturday _____ _____

2. We drove to a quarry and looked for fossils _____ _____

3. What cool fossils _____ _____

4. This one is a trilobite _____ _____

5. Don't drop it _____ _____

6. Next time we go, you should come with us _____ _____

7. Will you tell me when you plan to go again _____ _____

B. Writing Application: *Write a short dialogue between two characters. Use at least one of each kind of sentence. Label your sentences* dec *for declarative,* int *for interrogative,* imp *for imperative, and* exclam *for exclamatory.*

_____

_____

_____

_____

"The Monsters Are Due on Maple Street" by Rod Serling
Integrated Language Skills: Support for Writing a Summary

A **summary** is a brief statement that presents only the main ideas and most important details of a literary work. Summarizing helps you review and understand what you are reading.

To summarize, you must first distinguish between important and unimportant details. Ask yourself questions like the following:

- Is this detail necessary for my understanding of the literary work?

- Would the literary work hold together without this information?

Use the following chart to take notes for your summary of Act 1 or Act 2 of the screenplay. Fill in the left-hand column first. Finish this column by stating the theme, or underlying meaning, of the act. Then, go through the right-hand column, and verify that each fact you are including reflects the act's meaning.

	Supports Underlying Meaning?
Main Idea #1:	(Y/N)
Supporting Detail:	(Y/N)
Supporting Detail:	(Y/N)
Supporting Detail:	(Y/N)
Main Idea #2	(Y/N)
Supporting Detail:	(Y/N)
Supporting Detail:	(Y/N)
Supporting Detail:	(Y/N)
Underlying Meaning:	

Now, write a draft of your summary. Include only those ideas and supporting details that reflect the underlying meaning of the screenplay.

"The Monsters Are Due on Maple Street" by Rod Serling
Integrated Language Skills: Support for Extend Your Learning

Research and Technology

Use this worksheet as you plan how you would **film the scene** you just presented.

Events that take place in the scene: _____

_____

_____

_____

_____

Camera angles that best capture each event: _____

_____

_____

_____

_____

When and how special effects should be used: _____

_____

_____

_____

_____

_____

Name _____ Date _____

The Monsters Are Due on Maple Street by Rod Serling
Open-Book Test

Short Answer *Write your responses to the questions in this section on the lines provided.*

1. The characters in Act I of Rod Serling's screenplay, *The Monsters Are Due on Maple Street,* get flustered. What event causes them to get flustered? How do they feel? Base your answer on the meaning of *flustered.*

   _____

   _____

2. In the middle of Act I of *The Monsters Are Due on Maple Street,* Steve talks about meteors and sunspots to explain the flash of light. What motivates him to make this explanation?

   _____

   _____

3. In the middle of Act I of *The Monsters Are Due on Maple Street,* the neighbors consider the possibility that one of them is responsible for the strange events. At what point does this happen? Why?

   _____

   _____

   _____

4. What is the main idea III Act I of *The Monsters Are Due on Maple Street?* What are two or three of the most important details of Act I? Use this information to write a one- or two-sentence summary of Act I.

   _____

   _____

5. One detail from the middle of Act II of *The Monsters Are Due on Maple Street* is that Charlie believes Pete Van Horn is a monster and shoots him. Why is this detail essential to an understanding of the play?

   _____

   _____

6. What emotions motivate the speakers in this passage from the middle of Act II of *The Monsters Are Due on Maple Street?* Explain.

   WOMAN. [*In a very hushed voice*] Charlie . . . Charlie . . . the lights just went on in your house. Why did the lights just go on?

   DON. What about it, Charlie? How come you're the only one with lights now?

   GOODMAN. That's what I'd like to know.

   _____

   _____

Unit 5 Resources: Drama
103

7. At the end of *The Monsters Are Due on Maple Street,* Figure One says that Maple Street is not unique and claims that they will go from one Maple Street to another "and let them destroy themselves." How do the events of the story prove Figure One's point?

_____

_____

_____

_____

8. In the chart below, write a motivation, or reason, for each character's action in *The Monsters Are Due on Maple Street.* Then, answer the questions that follow.

Action	Motivation
Early in Act I, Steve offers to go downtown.	
Toward the end of Act I, Sally points out that Goodman's car started by itself.	
Toward the end of Act II, Charlie runs into his house	

Which character's action is motivated because he or she wants something?

_____

What does this character want? _____

9. What kind of metamorphosis do the people of Maple Street undergo in *The Monsters Are Due on Maple Street?* Base your answer on the meaning of *metamorphosis.*

_____

_____

_____

10. Do the monsters ever come to Maple Street? Who are the real monsters in *The Monsters Are Due on Maple Street?*

_____

_____

_____

Essay

Write an extended response to the question of your choice or to the question or questions your teacher assigns you.

11. In Act I of *The Monsters Are Due on Maple Street,* Tommy tells a story about aliens. After hearing the story, Steve says they had better "run a check on the neighborhood and see which ones of us are really human." Is Steve being serious or is he making a humorous comment? In an essay, discuss two emotions that might have motivated Steve to make that comment.

12. The stage directions at the end of *The Monsters Are Due on Maple Street* note that Figure One and Figure Two cannot be clearly seen. Do you think the Figures are aliens, monsters, human beings, or something else? In an essay, tell what you think was the cause of the mysterious events on Maple Street. Then, describe how you imagine the Figures. Explain why the Figures look as you imagine them.

13. In an essay, describe how the screenplay of *The Monsters Are Due on Maple Street* illustrates the dangers of mob mentality. Why does this kind of thinking often lead to violence? What part do fear and suspicion play in creating a mob mentality?

14. **Thinking About the Big Question: Do others see us more clearly than we see ourselves?** In *The Monsters Are Due on Maple Street,* the people of Maple Street become gradually less able to see one another as they really are. In an essay, explain what causes their inability to see their neighbors clearly. Use details from the play to support your answer.

Oral Response

15. Go back to question 2, 5, or 7 or the question your teacher assigns you. Take a few minutes to expand your answer and prepare an oral response. Find additional details in "The Monsters Are Due on Maple Street" that support your points. If necessary, make notes to guide your oral response.

"The Monsters Are Due on Maple Street" by Rod Serling
Selection Test A

Critical Reading *Identify the letter of the choice that best answers the question.*

____ 1. In Act I of "The Monsters Are Due on Maple Street," which event signals the beginning of the town's troubles?
A. A woman's telephone does not work.
B. A man's electric mower will not start.
C. A roar is heard, and a flash of light is seen.
D. A boy tells about some stories he has read.

____ 2. In Act I of "The Monsters Are Due on Maple Street," what motivates Steve to explain the flash of light by talking about meteors and sunspots?
A. He knows a lot about science and wants to educate his neighbors.
B. He wants to reassure himself that there is nothing to fear.
C. He is from outer space and wants to act like a human being.
D. He wants to find the meteor and sell it to a collector.

____ 3. In Act I of "The Monsters Are Due on Maple Street," Tommy makes some suggestions about the events that are causing fear on Maple Street. Which suggestions does he make?
  I.   People from outer space are responsible.
  II. Some people on Maple Street are from outer space.
  III. Mr. Goodman is from outer space.
  IV. Nobody should try to leave the town.
A. I, II, IV
B. II, III, IV
C. I, III, IV
D. I, II, III

____ 4. In Act I of "The Monsters Are Due on Maple Street," what is Steve's motivation for asking Tommy to explain his story about the aliens sent ahead to earth?
A. He wants to make Tommy look foolish.
B. He wants to know what Tommy thinks.
C. He wants to take charge of the action.
D. He wants to leave town immediately.

____ 5. Which of these events in Act I of "The Monsters Are Due on Maple Street" is a clue that the neighbors will stop trusting one another?

    A. Don suggests that an electrical storm has caused the power to go off.

    B. A woman says that Tommy has been reading too many comic books.

    C. A man says that they should not be paying attention to Tommy.

    D. Steve jokes that they should check to see who among them is human.

____ 6. Which of these details would not be important in a summary of the action of Act I of "The Monsters Are Due on Maple Street"?

    A. Pete Van Horn is tall and thin.

    B. Electric appliances stop working.

    C. Neighbors wonder who among them is an alien.

    D. Tommy says that no one should leave town.

____ 7. Which of these is the best summary of Act I of "The Monsters Are Due on Maple Street"?

    A. The neighbors on Maple Street are unhappy because their power is out.

    B. Les Goodman frightens his neighbors when his car starts by itself.

    C. A strange event causes neighbors to become suspicious of one another.

    D. Pete Van Horn leaves Maple Street to see what is happening elsewhere.

____ 8. In Act II of "The Monsters Are Due on Maple Street," what role does Steve play as his neighbors keep watch on the Goodmans' house?

    A. He acts as the hanging judge: He tries to convince them that Goodman is dangerous.

    B. He acts as executioner: He volunteers for a firing squad to execute the guilty parties.

    C. He acts as peacemaker: He tries to persuade his neighbors to put aside their suspicions.

    D. He acts as spy: He tries to reach the aliens on his ham radio.

____ 9. What emotion motivates Steve in this speech from Act II of "The Monsters Are Due on Maple Street"?

> Go ahead, what's my wife said? Let's get it all out. Let's pick out every idiosyncrasy of every single man, woman, and child on the street. And then we might as well set up some kind of kangaroo court. How about a firing squad at dawn, Charlie, so we can get rid of all the suspects?

    A. disgust

    B. amusement

    C. sorrow

    D. love

_____ 10. Who or what are the monsters in the title "The Monsters Are Due on Maple Street"?

    A. the people who live on Maple Street

    B. the electric appliances on Maple Street

    C. Les and Ethel Goodman

    D. Figures One and Two

Vocabulary and Grammar

_____ 11. In which sentence is the meaning of the word *flustered* suggested?

    A. That was the way they prepared things for the landing.

    B. He always was an oddball. Him and his whole family.

    C. I don't understand. I swear . . . I don't understand.

    D. They pick the most dangerous enemy they can find.

_____ 12. Which of these sentences is declarative?

    A. It was an eventful night on Maple Street.

    B. Was it an eventful night on Maple Street?

    C. Observe the eventful night on Maple Street.

    D. What an eventful night it was on Maple Street!

Essay

13. In Act I of "The Monsters Are Due on Maple Street," after he has heard Tommy's story about the aliens, Steve makes this comment:

> Well, I guess what we'd better do then is to run a check on the neighborhood and see which ones of us are really human.

In an essay, discuss two emotions that might have motivated Steve to make that comment.

14. The stage directions at the end of "The Monsters Are Due on Maple Street" note that Figures One and Two cannot be clearly seen. If you were directing the play, would you depict the figures as aliens, as monsters, or as human beings? In an essay, describe how you would depict the figures, and explain the reasons for your choice. Include one detail from the play to support your explanation.

15. **Thinking About the Big Question: Do others see us more clearly than we see ourselves?** In "The Monsters Are Due on Maple Street," the people of Maple Street grow less and less able to see each other as they really are. In an essay, explain why they can no longer see their neighbors clearly. Use details from the play to support your answer.

"The Monsters Are Due on Maple Street" by Rod Serling
Selection Test B

Critical Reading *Identify the letter of the choice that best completes the statement or answers the question.*

_____ 1. Which event in "The Monsters Are Due on Maple Street" starts the breakdown of the community?
A. the voices of Figure One and Figure Two
B. the sound of an object passing overhead
C. an argument between Steve and Charlie
D. a story told by Tommy about space aliens

_____ 2. In Act I of "The Monsters Are Due on Maple Street," what motivates Steve to identify meteors and sunspots as the source of the neighborhood's troubles?
A. He is an astronomy teacher.
B. He is an alien disguised as a human.
C. He wants to reassure the neighbors.
D. He wants to excavate the meteor.

_____ 3. In Act I of "The Monsters Are Due on Maple Street," at what point do the neighbors begin to consider the possibility that one of them is responsible for the strange events?
A. when Pete Van Horn says that he is going to see if the power is still on on Floral Street
B. when Tommy says that aliens resembling humans are sent ahead to prepare for a landing
C. when Steve talks about meteors and sunspots as the most likely explanation
D. when Steve and Charlie decide that they will walk downtown to talk to the police

_____ 4. Which of these details is unimportant to a summary of Act I of "The Monsters Are Due on Maple Street"?
A. Phones and various machines stop working.
B. A large object flashes overhead and disappears.
C. Steve has recently filled his car's gas tank.
D. Tommy says that no one should leave the town.

_____ 5. What emotion motivates Steve to make this speech in Act II of "The Monsters Are Due on Maple Street"?

There's something you can do, Charlie. You could go home and keep your mouth shut. You could quit strutting around like a self-appointed hanging judge and just climb into bed and forget it.

A. optimism
B. fury
C. love
D. boredom

____ 6. Which of these statements would be unimportant in a summary of Act I?
   A. A roar and a flash of light interrupt the usual events in a neighborhood one
      evening.
   B. The power fails, telephones and portable radios do not work, and cars will
      not start.
   C. A boy says that the aliens would not like it if the neighbors left the town.
   D. A man reminds his neighbors that his family has lived on the street for five years.

____ 7. In Act II of "The Monsters Are Due on Maple Street," why are the residents so quick
   to focus on one another as the source of their fear?
   A. They have never trusted one another.
   B. They want to keep the focus off themselves.
   C. They have evidence that there are aliens in the town.
   D. They see that some neighbors have lights and some do not.

____ 8. Which detail from Act II of "The Monsters Are Due on Maple Street" is essential to
   an understanding of the play?
   A. Sally says that she and Ethel Goodman have been friends for years.
   B. Steve says that no one may enter his home without a search warrant.
   C. Charlie believes that Pete Van Horn is a monster and shoots him.
   D. The lights in Charlie's house suddenly come back on.

____ 9. What emotion motivates the speakers in this passage from Act II of "The Monsters
   Are Due on Maple Street"?
   > WOMAN. [*In a very hushed voice*] Charlie . . . Charlie . . . the lights just went on in your
   > house. Why did the lights just go on?
   >
   > DON. What about it, Charlie? How come you're the only one with lights now?
   >
   > GOODMAN. That's what I'd like to know.

   A. suspicion
   B. anger
   C. sympathy
   D. despair

____ 10. At the climax of "The Monsters Are Due on Maple Street," what single message
   underlies all of the characters' statements?
   A. Pick on them, not on me!
   B. I want my lights back on!
   C. I never believed in aliens!
   D. Somebody, call the police!

____ 11. What can you conclude from the dialogue between Figures One and Two at the
   conclusion of "The Monsters Are Due on Maple Street"?
   A. This is not the first town they have visited.
   B. They know how to control meteors and sunspots.
   C. They will settle on Maple Street as human beings.
   D. They are successful only in small towns.

____ 12. Which of these lines best expresses the theme of "The Monsters Are Due on Maple Street"?
   A. "I was just tryin' to . . . tryin' to protect my home, that's all!"
   B. "Maybe Peter there was trying to tell us something."
   C. "No . . . no . . . it's nothing of the sort! I don't know why the lights are on."
   D. "They pick the most dangerous enemy they can find . . . and it's themselves."

Vocabulary and Grammar

____ 13. In which sentence is the meaning of the word *sluggishly* suggested?
   A. My brother shuffled into the room and slumped into a chair.
   B. Her aunt prepared for the tournament by working out every day.
   C. His sister worked at her computer until she had finished her paper.
   D. The adventurers rafted through the dangerous white-water rapids.

____ 14. In which sentence is the meaning of the word *defiant* suggested?
   A. Well, why don't you go downtown and check with the police.
   B. Go ahead, Tommy. What kind of story was this?
   C. It's just a ham radio set. A lot of people have them.
   D. If they want to look inside our house—let them get a search warrant.

____ 15. Which of these sentences is imperative?
   A. Operator, operator, something's wrong on the phone, operator!
   B. Well, why don't you go downtown and check with the police.
   C. Come over here and stop that kind of talk.
   D. Charlie, there's a dead man on the sidewalk and you killed him!

Essay

16. When the neighbors begin to suspect Charlie in "The Monsters Are Due on Maple Street," he runs toward his house, and the neighbors chase him. Charlie then declares that the "monster" is Tommy. In an essay, explain why Charlie makes this accusation. Then, explain why the neighbors are ready to believe him.

17. As you were reading "The Monsters Are Due On Maple Street," what did you think had caused the mysterious events—the roar and the flash, the power outage, the dead phones and radios, the cars that would not start and then started on their own? In an essay, describe what you believed was the cause of the events. When you read the end of the play, when the space craft and vaguely seen figures are described, what did you think? Did the ending change your ideas? Why or why not?

18. **Thinking About the Big Question: Do others see us more clearly than we see ourselves?** In "The Monsters Are Due on Maple Street," the people of Maple Street become gradually less able to see each other as they really are. In an essay, explain what causes their inability to see their neighbors clearly. Use details from the play to support your answer.

Vocabulary Warm-up Word Lists

Study these words from the selections. Then, complete the activities.

Word List A

announced [uh NOWNST] *v.* said; officially told people that something would happen
The principal <u>announced</u> that school would be closed next week.

appetite [AP uh tyt] *n.* hunger; desire for food
The smell of my grandmother's cooking always gives me an <u>appetite</u>.

contribute [kuhn TRIB yoot] *v.* give to a cause or group effort
The movie star asked everyone to <u>contribute</u> to the food drive.

decent [DEE suhnt] *adj.* good; suitable; satisfactory
A <u>decent</u> meal fills you up.

fines [FYNZ] *n.* money paid as punishment
The driver had to pay $150 in <u>fines</u> for parking illegally.

fund [FUHND] *n.* money set aside for a specific purpose
Marie's grandparents established a <u>fund</u> to pay for her education.

items [EYE tuhmz] *n.* things that are grouped together
Of all the <u>items</u> on the menu, Dave liked the sandwiches best.

notices [NOH tis iz] *n.* printed messages telling of an event or giving a warning
Maggie put up <u>notices</u> all around the school to announce the dance.

Word List B

critical [KRIT i kuhl] *adj.* very important; necessary
To pass the test, it is <u>critical</u> that you study first.

fascinating [FAS uh nayt ing] *adj.* very interesting; holding someone's attention
Peter found the dinosaur exhibit <u>fascinating</u> and spent an hour there.

frantically [FRAN tik lee] *adv.* in a panic; wildly
When the bus came, I looked frantically for my ticket but could not find it.

hollow [HAHL oh] *adj.* having a space inside
The chocolate rabbit was <u>hollow</u> and easy to break apart.

immigrants [IM uh gruhnts] *n.* people who come into a new country to settle there
Many Irish <u>immigrants</u> came to America during the potato famine.

stranded [STRAND id] *v.* stuck someplace without a way back
After the shipwreck, the sailor was <u>stranded</u> on a desert island.

swindle [SWIN duhl] *n.* trick; an act or plan that cheats someone
They tried to sell him a broken-down car, but he knew the deal was a <u>swindle</u>.

topple [TAHP uhl] *v.* overturn; tip over
One of the legs of the chair is broken, so it will <u>topple</u> over if you sit on it.

Name _____ Date _____

from **Grandpa and the Statue** by Arthur Miller
"My Head Is Full of Starshine" by Peg Kehret
Vocabulary Warm-up Exercises

Exercise A *Fill in each blank in the paragraph below with an appropriate word from Word List A. Use each word only once.*

Joyce liked to study in the library because the library computers were in

[1] _____ condition and did not crash. She could also use the books

without checking them out. That way, she did not have to worry about paying

[2] _____ if she forgot to return them on time. When she wanted to

stretch, she stood and read the [3] _____ on the bulletin boards. Some of

the [4] _____ hanging there caught her interest. One sign

[5] _____ that a local hospital was collecting money and toys for a holi-

day [6] _____. Joyce was looking for a place to donate her stuffed ani-

mals and wanted to [7] _____.

There was only one problem; no one was allowed to eat in the library. Somehow, know-

ing that gave Joyce an [8] _____. She was hungry when she got home!

Exercise B *Answer each question. Explain how the meaning of the underlined word led you to answer as you did.*

Example: Which is more valuable, a <u>hollow</u> gold bar or a solid one of the same size?
The solid one is more valuable. The <u>hollow</u> one has a space in the middle, so it contains less gold than the solid one would have.

1. If your friend's help is <u>critical</u> to your plan, will you ask him or her to help you?

   _____

2. If you find chess <u>fascinating</u>, would you enjoy watching a game?

   _____

3. If you are looking <u>frantically</u> for your keys, are you searching in a calm, orderly way?

   _____

4. Have new <u>immigrants</u> to the United States lived here all their lives?

   _____

5. If someone is <u>stranded</u> in the woods, what should the person do to get help?

   _____

6. If you found out that a deal someone offered you was a <u>swindle</u>, what might you do?

   _____

7. If buildings <u>topple</u> over in a strong wind, were they built well?

   _____

Unit 5 Resources: Drama
© Pearson Education, Inc. All rights reserved.
113

Name _____   Date _____

from **Grandpa and the Statue** by Arthur Miller
"My Head Is Full of Starshine" by Peg Kehret
Reading Warm-up A

Read the following passage. Pay special attention to the underlined words. Then, complete the activities. Use a separate sheet of paper for your written answers.

Janie and Deanna decided to start a club to collect money for a charitable <u>fund</u>. Kids could <u>contribute</u> dollars, or they could give their time and help out at club events. Janie, the practical one, made notes as she and Deanna thought of ways to encourage their friends to join.

Deanna, the creative one, <u>announced</u> that she had already thought of a name. "Let's call it 'The Buzz Club,'" she said. She liked the idea of her friends buzzing around, helping people. She even wanted club members to call themselves the Busy Bees. However, Janie thought the idea was corny.

"It is cute, not corny," Deanna argued. "Each member could wear a pin shaped like a bee or a hive."

"Boys don't usually wear pins," Janie said. "Let's discuss it at our first meeting and vote on the name." Then, she looked at the <u>items</u> on her To-do List. "Where should we get together?"

"The diner on Eighth Street is a good place," Deanna offered. "They have big tables and <u>decent</u> food, and I like being in a diner because talking gives me an <u>appetite</u>."

"Maybe a diner isn't the best place," Janie thought aloud. "Kids might not come if they think they have to buy something."

"Well, there's the conference room in the library. We don't need money there except to pay <u>fines</u> for overdue books."

"Good point," Janie agreed. "Now, all we need are <u>notices</u> telling people when and where to go for the first meeting."

"I'll make them," Deanna said. "I've got some great design ideas."

Janie smiled. "Okay. Just promise me: no bees!"

Deanna laughed. "I promise," she said. She wondered how such opposite people could be such great friends!

1. Underline the word that tells what goes in a <u>fund</u>. Then, tell what a *fund* is.

2. Circle the word in the sentence that means almost the same as <u>contribute</u>. Then, name a cause to which you might like to *contribute*.

3. Underline the words that tell what Deanna <u>announced</u>. If Deanna *announced* something, did she keep it a secret? Explain how you know.

4. Circle the words that tell where the <u>items</u> appeared. List two other items that might appear there.

5. Underline the word that tells what Deanna thinks is <u>decent</u>. Tell about a place you know where this thing is *decent*.

6. Circle the word that tells what gives Deanna an <u>appetite</u>. What gives you an *appetite*?

7. Underline the words that describe what kind of <u>fines</u> you pay in a library. Name other kinds of *fines*.

8. Circle the words that tell the purpose of the <u>notices</u>. If you made these *notices*, which words would you write in the biggest letters?

from **Grandpa and the Statue** by Arthur Miller
"My Head Is Full of Starshine" by Peg Kehret
Reading Warm-up B

Read the following passage. Pay special attention to the underlined words. Then, complete the activities. Use a separate sheet of paper for your written answers.

According to the writer Somerset Maugham, "There are three rules for writing a novel. Unfortunately, no one knows what they are." In other words, writing is a complicated art. Some writers struggle to come up with an opening sentence, <u>frantically</u> trying one idea after another in their desperation. If they run out of ideas, they feel <u>hollow</u> inside. Writing is difficult to master. However, most writers agree that to write well, a person must (1) have something to say, (2) stick to the point, and (3) be truthful.

Having something to say requires thinking. Writers need to ask themselves what their main character wants and what is preventing him or her from getting it. If a writer cannot supply the answers, the character will be <u>stranded</u> in the middle of the story.

Once the writer begins writing, he or she must stick to the point. A story is like a tall, well-balanced building. If a story has too many different parts, it may <u>topple</u> over and come crashing to the ground. It is <u>critical</u> to know in advance where the story is headed. Writers who do not have any idea where the story will lead may be headed for disaster.

Truth and honesty add power to stories. For this reason, many authors write about their own experiences. For example, <u>immigrants</u> often describe the adjustments they had to make when moving to a new country. Readers may find these stories <u>fascinating</u> and hard to put down.

Whatever the subject matter, there is usually a deeper message the writer hopes to convey. If the message rings true, the writer will touch the reader's mind and heart. If there is no truth in it, then the reader will feel cheated, as if the book is a <u>swindle</u>.

1. Underline the phrase that is a clue to the meaning of <u>frantically</u>. Describe the opposite of working *frantically*.

2. Circle the words that tell why writers might feel <u>hollow</u> inside. Describe something *hollow*.

3. Underline the words that explain where a character might become <u>stranded</u>. What does *stranded* mean?

4. Circle the phrase that is a clue to the meaning of <u>topple</u>. Explain how to make sure something does not *topple*.

5. Underline the words that tell what it is <u>critical</u> to know in advance. Then, name something that is *critical*.

6. Circle the words that are a clue to the meaning of <u>immigrants</u>. How do people become *immigrants*?

7. Underline the words that are a clue to the meaning of <u>fascinating</u>. Then, name something *fascinating*.

8. Circle the word that is a clue to the meaning of <u>swindle</u>. Then, describe the type of person who is *not* likely to be the victim of a *swindle*.

Name _____ Date _____

from **Grandpa and the Statue** by Arthur Miller
"My Head Is Full of Starshine" by Peg Kehret
Writing About the Big Question
Do others see us more clearly than we see ourselves?

Big Question Vocabulary

appearance	appreciate	assumption	bias	characteristic
define	focus	identify	ignore	image
perception	perspective	reaction	reflect	reveal

A. *Choose one word from the list above to complete each sentence. There may be more than one right answer.*

1. Some musicians work very hard to create the right _____ for their band.

2. An older person's _____ on a problem may be different than a child's.

3. What we see, smell, taste, hear and feel adds up to our _____ of the world.

B. *Follow the directions in responding to each of the items below.*

1. List at least two different ways people may get the wrong impression of another person. Write your response in complete sentences.

   _____

   _____

2. If you could see yourself as other do, would you want to? Write at least three sentences explaining your position. Use at least two of the Big Question vocabulary words. You may use the words in different forms (for example you can change *reflect* to *reflection*).

   _____

   _____

C. *Complete the sentence below. Then, write a short paragraph in which you connect this sentence to the big question.*

   The best way to understand a person is to _____

   _____

   _____

Name _____ Date _____

from **Grandpa and the Statue** by Arthur Miller
"My Head Is Full of Starshine" by Peg Kehret
Literary Analysis: Comparing Dramatic Speeches

Dramatic speeches are performed by actors in a drama or play. Whether spoken by a character who is onstage alone or given by a character who is part of a larger scene, these speeches move the action of the story forward and help define the conflict in a play. There are two main types of dramatic speeches:

- **Monologues** are long, uninterrupted speeches that are spoken by a single character. They reveal the private thoughts and feelings of the character.
- **Dialogues** are conversations between characters. They reveal characters' traits, develop conflict, and move the plot forward.

Grandpa and the Statue is a dialogue, and "My Head Is Full of Starshine" is a monologue. As you read these selections, consider what you learn about the characters. Also, think about how other key information is revealed.

DIRECTIONS: *Answer the following questions about the excerpts from* Grandpa and the Statue *and "My Head Is Full of Starshine."*

1. In the excerpt from *Grandpa and the Statue,* what does the audience learn about Monaghan's character?

   _____

   _____

2. What conflict is revealed in Monaghan and Sheean's dialogue in the excerpt from *Grandpa and the Statue?*

   _____

   _____

3. In the excerpt from *Grandpa and the Statue,* what does Monaghan reveal about himself in the speech about his experiences when he first came to America?

   _____

   _____

4. How does the reader learn about the writer's tendency to daydream in "My Head Is Full of Starshine"?

   _____

   _____

5. What does the writer reveal about her feelings toward having library fines in "My Head Is Full of Starshine"?

   _____

   _____

from **Grandpa and the Statue** by Arthur Miller
"My Head Is Full of Starshine" by Peg Kehret

Vocabulary Builder

Word List

peeved   potential   practical   rummaging

A. DIRECTIONS: *Read each sentence, paying attention to the italicized word from the Word List. Then, answer each question, and explain your answer.*

1. If you accidentally threw away a diamond ring, might you be *rummaging* through the trash?

   _____

2. Is a *practical* person one who daydreams and puts things off until the last minute?

   _____

3. Is a relaxed, easygoing person likely to be easily *peeved*?

   _____

4. Is someone with great *potential* as an athlete likely to compete in the Olympics someday?

   _____

B. DIRECTIONS: *Write the letter of the word whose meaning is* most like *that of the word from the Word List.*

____ 1. peeved
   A. outgoing   B. happy   C. realistic   D. annoyed

____ 2. practical
   A. happy   B. realistic   C. strong   D. imaginative

____ 3. rummaging
   A. reselling   B. organizing   C. searching   D. destroying

____ 4. potential
   A. capability   B. intelligence   C. sharpness   D. volume

Name _____ Date _____

from **Grandpa and the Statue** by Arthur Miller
"My Head Is Full of Starshine" by Peg Kehret
Support for Writing to Compare Dramatic Speeches

Use this graphic organizer to take notes for your essay comparing and contrasting the dramatic speech by Monaghan in the excerpt from *Grandpa and the Statue* with the one by the speaker in "My Head Is Full of Starshine."

Which ideas in the speech are familiar to you?_____
_____
_____
_____
_____

With which ideas in the speech do you agree or disagree?_____
_____
_____
_____
_____

Which character do you relate to more? Why?
_____
_____
_____
_____
_____
_____
_____

The speaker in "My Head Is Full of Starshine"

Monaghan in *Grandpa and the Statue*

From which character do you think you learn more? Why?_____
_____
_____
_____
_____
_____
_____

Which ideas in the speech are familiar to you?_____
_____
_____
_____
_____

With which ideas in the speech do you agree or disagree?_____
_____
_____
_____
_____

Now, use your notes to write a draft of an essay comparing and contrasting the two speeches.

from **Grandpa and the Statue** by Arthur Miller and
"My Head Is Full of Starshine" by Peg Kehret
Open-Book Test

Short Answer *Write your responses to the questions in this section on the lines provided.*

1. At the beginning of the excerpt from *Grandpa and the Statue*, Monaghan says, "Oh, that," when Sheean starts talking about the Statue of Liberty fund. What does Monaghan mean when he says that?

   _____

   _____

   _____

2. In the middle of *Grandpa and the Statue,* Sheean says the date in Roman numbers that is written on the tablet of the Statue of Liberty is "very high class." What does this tell you about him?

   _____

   _____

   _____

3. In the middle of *Grandpa and the Statue,* Monaghan does not like what is written on the tablet. He thinks it should just say "Welcome All." Why does he think it should be changed?

   _____

   _____

   _____

4. Toward the end of *Grandpa and the Statue*, Monaghan gives a speech about his early experiences in America. What does his speech reveal about him?

   _____

   _____

   _____

5. Throughout "My Head Is Full of Starshine," the speaker describes her friend Pam. What purpose does her description serve? Explain.

   _____

   _____

   _____

6. Would Mr. Evans, the science teacher mentioned in the middle of "My Head Is Full of Starshine," prefer the speaker or Pam as a student? Why?

   _____

   _____

Name _____ Date _____

7. At the end of "My Head Is Full of Starshine," the speaker says, "My head Is full of starshine." Can the same be said about Monaghan in *Grandpa and the Statue*? Why or why not?

_____

_____

_____

_____

8. How does Pam feel about the speaker in "My Head Is Full of Starshine"? Does Sheean in *Grandpa and the Statue* feel the same way about Monaghan? How do you know?

_____

_____

_____

_____

9. Does the speaker in "My Head Is Full of Starshine" work to her potential in science class? Base your answer on the meaning of *potential*.

_____

_____

_____

_____

10. A dramatic speech can reveal a character's traits. In the chart below, write two character traits that are revealed by each character's dramatic speeches in *Grandpa and the Statue* and in "My Head Is Full of Starshine." Then, answer the question that follows the chart.

Character	Traits
Monaghan	
Sheean	
Speaker	

Which character do you think is the most admirable? Why?_____

_____

Essay

Write an extended response to the question of your choice or to the question or questions your teacher assigns you.

11. In an essay, define monologue and dialogue. Then, tell which of the two selections, the excerpt from *Grandpa and the Statue* or "My Head Is Full of Starshine," is a monologue and which is a dialogue. Cite details from each work that help characterize it as one kind of dramatic speech or the other.

12. Both Monaghan in the excerpt from *Grandpa and the Statue* and the speaker in "My Head Is Full of Starshine" give dramatic speeches. In an essay, compare and contrast Monaghan's speech about his first experiences in New York with the opening of "My Head Is Full of Starshine," in which the speaker compares Pam's preparations for a party with her own. Tell why each speaker is giving the speech. Explain what you learn about each speaker from the speech. Use details and examples from the speeches to support your response.

13. Both the excerpt from *Grandpa and the Statue* and "My Head Is Full of Starshine" focus on a relationship between two people. In an essay, compare the relationship between Sheean and Monaghan with the relationship between the speaker in "My Head Is Full of Starshine" and Pam. What is the conflict in each relationship? How is it resolved? Conclude your essay by telling which relationship you found most interesting, and why.

14. **Thinking About the Big Question: Do others see us more clearly than we see ourselves?** Monaghan in *Grandpa and the Statue* and the speaker in "My Head Is Full of Starshine" have relationships with people who see them differently from the way they see themselves. In an essay, tell how Sheean sees Monaghan or how Pam sees the speaker. Does the friend see the character clearly? Does he or she see things about the character that the character does not see? Use details from the dramatic speech you choose to support your response.

Oral Response

15. Go back to question 4, 7, or 8 or to the question your teacher assigns you. Take a few minutes to expand your answer and prepare an oral response. Find additional details in *Grandpa and the Statue* or "My Head Is Full of Starshine" that support your points. If necessary, make notes to guide your oral response.

from Grandpa and the Statue by Arthur Miller
"My Head Is Full of Starshine" by Peg Kehret
Selection Test A

Critical Reading *Identify the letter of the choice that best answers the question.*

____ 1. In the excerpt from *Grandpa and the Statue,* what does Sheean ask Monaghan to do?
   A. go with him on a boat to see the Statue of Liberty
   B. donate money for the Statue of Liberty's base
   C. help him convince the neighbors to donate money
   D. pay for a trolley ride to see the Statue of Liberty

____ 2. What do these words of Monaghan's from *Grandpa and the Statue* reveal about him?

   I'm not throwin' me good money away for something I don't even know exists.

   A. He is foolish and uneducated.
   B. He is wise and careful.
   C. He is cheap and suspicious.
   D. He is patient and hardworking.

____ 3. In *Grandpa and the Statue,* why does Sheean take Monaghan to the warehouse?
   A. Monaghan wants to see the statue's base while it is being built.
   B. Sheean wants Monaghan to talk to the people who built the statue.
   C. Sheean wants time with Monaghan to convince him to donate money.
   D. Monaghan wants to see the statue to make sure it actually exists.

____ 4. In *Grandpa and the Statue,* why doesn't Monaghan like what is written on the statue?
   A. He believes it should just say, "Welcome All."
   B. He doesn't understand Roman numerals.
   C. He thinks people will have trouble reading it.
   D. He understands that history is important to people.

____ 5. In *Grandpa and the Statue,* what does Monaghan's refusal to give a donation reveal about him?
   A. He is very stubborn.
   B. He is an angry person.
   C. He is easily swayed.
   D. He has very little money.

_____ 6. In *Grandpa and the Statue,* what can you tell about Sheean from his discussion with Monaghan?

   A. He is easily angered and impatient.

   B. He is patriotic and generous.

   C. He is friendly and casual.

   D. He is mysterious and quiet.

_____ 7. What aspect of the excerpt from *Grandpa and the Statue* makes it a dialogue?

   A. It is a conversation between characters.

   B. It is written in the form of a story.

   C. The characters' actions are described.

   D. The characters' thoughts are described.

_____ 8. According to the speaker in "My Head Is Full of Starshine," what does she do to get ready for Margo's party while Pam has been working on a dress to wear?

   A. She is choosing the outfit she will wear.

   B. She is writing a poem for Margo.

   C. She is working to pay for Margo's gift.

   D. She is trying to improve her science grade.

_____ 9. What school assignments does the speaker in "My Head Is Full of Starshine" most enjoy?

   A. studying insects

   B. reading about flying carpets

   C. writing essays or stories

   D. returning library books

_____ 10. What does the speaker in "My Head Is Full of Starshine" mean by this remark, which she makes at the end of the monologue?

   My head is full of starshine. Except for those library fines, I'm glad it is.

   A. She likes herself the way she is, for the most part.

   B. She plans to remember to return her books on time.

   C. She is glad that she is able to see stars at night.

   D. She likes writing, but she does not like reading.

_____ 11. What aspect of "My Head Is Full of Starshine" makes it a monologue?

   A. It is about only one topic.

   B. It is about one person's life.

   C. It characterizes only one person.

   D. It is spoken by only one character.

Vocabulary

____ 12. In which sentence might a character be said to be working up to her *potential*?

A. Pam makes a list of everything she plans to do the next day.

B. Pam pays attention in science class and gets an *A* for the term.

C. The speaker in "My Head Is Full of Starshine" forgets to return books on time.

D. The speaker in "My Head Is Full of Starshine" daydreams in science class.

____ 13. If someone is *rummaging* through a box, what is he or she doing?

A. destroying the contents

B. throwing out the contents

C. organizing the contents

D. looking through the contents

____ 14. Which sentence best describes someone who is *peeved*?

A. Sheean greets Monaghan and asks about his wife.

B. Sheean invites Monaghan to come with him to a warehouse.

C. Monaghan angrily refuses to give Sheean any money.

D. Sheean offers to give a dime to the fund for Monaghan.

Essay

15. Both Monaghan in the excerpt from *Grandpa and the Statue* and the speaker in "My Head Is Full of Starshine" give dramatic speeches. In an essay, compare and contrast Monaghan's speech in which he tells about his first experiences in New York with the opening of "My Head Is Full of Starshine," in which the speaker compares Pam's preparations for a party with her own. Tell why each speaker is giving the speech, and share what you learn about each speaker from the speech.

16. A monologue is a long speech given by one character; a dialogue is a conversation between two or more characters. In an essay, contrast the excerpt from *Grandpa and the Statue* with "My Head Is Full of Starshine." Explain how you can tell the difference between the one that is a monologue and the one that is a dialogue. Finally, tell which character you like best, and explain why.

17. **Thinking About the Big Question: Do others see us more clearly than we see ourselves?** Some people see Monaghan in *Grandpa and the Statue* and the speaker in "My Head Is Full of Starshine" differently from the way they see themselves. In an essay, tell how Sheean sees Monaghan or how Pam sees the speaker. Does the friend see the character clearly? Use details from the dramatic speech you choose to support your response.

from Grandpa and the Statue by Arthur Miller
"My Head Is Full of Starshine" by Peg Kehret
Selection Test B

Critical Reading *Identify the letter of the choice that best completes the statement or answers the question.*

_____ 1. What does this line from *Grandpa and the Statue* reveal about Sheean?

   SHEEAN. [*slight brogue*] A good afternoon to you, Monaghan.

   A. He is very kind.
   B. He likes to joke.
   C. He is from Ireland.
   D. He likes Monaghan.

_____ 2. In the excerpt from *Grandpa and the Statue*, why does Monaghan say, "Oh, that" when Sheean starts talking about the Statue of Liberty fund?
   A. He does not really want to discuss the matter.
   B. He has been waiting to talk to Sheean about it.
   C. He has no idea what Sheean is talking about.
   D. He wants to hear more information from Sheean.

_____ 3. In *Grandpa and the Statue*, which of the following do you find out about Monaghan from his dialogue with Sheean?
   A. He does not like Sheean and tries to avoid him.
   B. He is ashamed of being stingy and would like to change.
   C. He does not believe what he reads in the newspapers.
   D. He likes to ride on the Staten Island ferry.

_____ 4. In *Grandpa and the Statue*, why does Monaghan think the statue is broken?
   A. It has no base to stand on.
   B. It is hidden in a warehouse.
   C. He has not had a chance to see it.
   D. It has not been put together yet.

_____ 5. In *Grandpa and the Statue*, what does Monaghan's speech about his early experiences in America reveal about why he is so suspicious?
   A. He had no place to stay and had to go to a rooming house.
   B. Many people made fun of him because of his brogue.
   C. He was robbed when he first came to the country.
   D. He did not see the Statue of Liberty welcoming him.

_____ 6. What do you learn about Sheean in these lines from *Grandpa and the Statue*?

   SHEEAN. It's in Roman numbers. Very high class.

   A. He is good at math and numbers.
   B. He understands American history.
   C. He is easily impressed.
   D. He knows all about the Statue of Liberty.

_____ 7. What aspect of the excerpt from *Grandpa and the Statue* makes it a dialogue?
   A. The characters are seen in more than one location.
   B. There is a conflict between Monaghan and Sheean.
   C. Monaghan gives information about his early life.
   D. It consists of a conversation between two characters.

_____ 8. According to the speaker in "My Head Is Full of Starshine," what is practical about her friend Pam?
   A. She makes a list of what she needs to do the next day.
   B. She says that the speaker's head is "full of starshine."
   C. She is interested in ladybugs and other insects.
   D. She works very hard and gets *A*'s in science.

_____ 9. According to the speaker in "My Head Is Full of Starshine," how does Pam feel about her?
   A. Pam feels annoyed with her because she is scatterbrained and dreamy.
   B. Pam thinks that she is foolish because she writes meaningless poetry.
   C. Pam likes her because she, like Pam, is practical and well-organized.
   D. Pam accepts her as a friend even though she is different from Pam.

_____ 10. In "My Head Is Full of Starshine," in what way does the speaker's mother wish the speaker were more like Pam?
   A. Unlike Pam's room, her room is always messy.
   B. She forgets to bring notices home from school.
   C. Unlike Pam, she does poorly in science.
   D. She writes poetry instead of studying science.

_____ 11. Why would Mr. Evans, the science teacher in "My Head Is Full of Starshine," prefer Pam as a student to the speaker?
   A. Pam does not write poetry or stories.
   B. Pam always earns *A*'s, whereas the speaker earns *B*'s.
   C. Pam talks all about insects during lunchtime.
   D. Pam pays attention and finds the lessons fascinating.

_____ 12. What does this sentence from "My Head Is Full of Starshine" reveal about the speaker?
   When Mr. Evans talks about gross things like that, I pretend my chair is a flying carpet, and I watch myself fly out the window.

   A. The speaker does not like Mr. Evans.
   B. The speaker is more creative than scientific.
   C. The speaker has always been a poor student.
   D. The speaker likes fairy tales.

_____ 13. For what purpose does the speaker in "My Head Is Full of Starshine" describe her friend Pam?
   A. Pam is her best friend, and she wants to write about her.
   B. She longs to be more like Pam so she can please her mother.
   C. Discussing Pam's differences helps to reveal more about herself.
   D. She is annoyed with Pam because Pam is so different from her.

_____ **14.** What aspect of "My Head Is Full of Starshine" makes it a monologue?
  A. It is a long, uninterrupted speech spoken by a single character.
  B. It is spoken without any enthusiasm, in a dull tone of voice.
  C. It consists of a comparison of the speaker and another character.
  D. It is a dramatic speech that moves the action of the story forward.

Vocabulary and Grammar

_____ **15.** Which of the following characters is most likely *peeved*?
  A. Richard is always quick to offer praise or encouragement.
  B. Julio is touchy, irritated, and quick to answer angrily.
  C. John volunteers at a soup kitchen every Sunday morning.
  D. Mary is friendly only with people who can do favors for her.

_____ **16.** Which of the following characters is most clearly *practical*?
  A. Amanda is extremely funny and would like to be a stand-up comedian someday.
  B. Jose plans his menus ahead of time and makes a list of the ingredients he needs.
  C. Lisa began assembling her new lawn mower without reading the instructions.
  D. Evan helped Lisa with the lawn mower instead of studying for his science exam.

_____ **17.** Who would most likely be *rummaging*?
  A. someone who is late for dinner
  B. someone who is planning a party
  C. someone who is organizing a picnic
  D. someone who is looking for an item

Essay

18. In an essay, define a monologue and a dialogue, and then tell which of the two selections, the excerpt from *Grandpa and the Statue* or "My Head Is Full of Starshine," is a monologue and which is a dialogue. Cite two details from each work that help to characterize it as one kind of dramatic speech or the other.

19. Both the excerpt from *Grandpa and the Statue* and "My Head Is Full of Starshine" focus on a relationship between two people. In an essay, compare the relationship between Sheean and Monaghan with the relationship between the speaker in "My Head Is Full of Starshine" and Pam. What is the conflict in each relationship? How is it resolved? Conclude your essay by telling which relationship you found most interesting and why.

20. Thinking About the Big Question: Do others see us more clearly than we see ourselves?
Monaghan in *Grandpa and the Statue* and the speaker in "My Head Is Full of Starshine" have relationships with people who see them differently from the way they see themselves. In an essay, tell how Sheean sees Monaghan or how Pam sees the speaker. Does the friend see the character clearly? Does he or she see things about the character that the character does not see? Use details from the dramatic speech you choose to support your response.

Name _____ Date _____

Exposition: Cause-and-Effect Essay

Prewriting: Narrowing Your Topic

Use the following web to narrow your topic. Write your topic in the center, surround it
with subtopics, and list causes and effects connected to each subtopic.

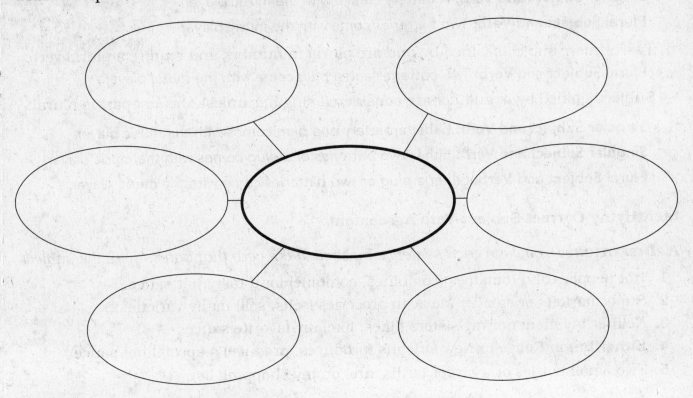

Drafting: Organizing Your Essay

List the main points of your cause-and-effect essay in the following graphic organizer.

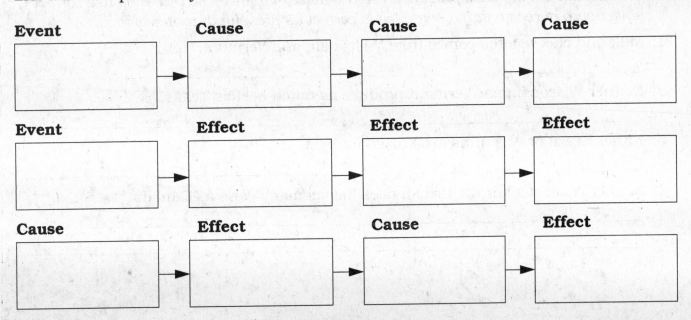

Writing Workshop—Unit 5, Part 2
Cause-and-Effect Essay: Integrating Grammar Skills

Revising for Subject-Verb Agreement with Compound Subjects

A verb must agree with its subject in **number**.

Singular Subject and Verb: A *battery comes* with the music player.

Plural Subject and Verb: Two *batteries come* with the music player.

Two or more subjects joined by *and* are plural in number and require a plural verb:
Plural Subject and Verb: Two *batteries and* a *plug come* with the music player.

Subjects joined by *or* and *nor* are considered singular unless the *last* part is plural.

Singular Subject and Verb: Either a *battery or* a *plug comes* with the music player.

Singular Subject and Verb: Either two *batteries or* a *plug comes* with the music player.

Plural Subject and Verb: Either a *plug or* two *batteries come* with the music player.

Identifying Correct Subject-Verb Agreement

A. DIRECTIONS: *Complete each sentence by circling the verb that agrees with the subject.*

1. Hot peppers and tomatoes (combines, combine) for a tasty hot sauce.
2. Supermarkets or smaller Mexican groceries (sells, sell) many varieties.
3. Neither my mom nor my sisters (likes, like) my favorite sauce.
4. Either Baton Rouge or New Orleans (produces, produce) a special hot sauce.
5. Two small bottles or a bigger jar (is, are) on my shopping list.

Fixing Incorrect Subject-Verb Agreement

B. DIRECTIONS: *On the lines provided, rewrite these sentences so that they use correct subject-verb agreement. If a sentence is correct as presented, write* correct.

1. Milk and cheese often comes from Wisconsin and Vermont.

_____

2. Neither Wisconsin nor Vermont produce as much beef as Texas.

_____

3. Either Brazil or Argentina are known for beef.

_____

4. Neither Australia nor the British Isles has as many cows as Canada.

_____

_____

Unit 5 Vocabulary Workshop—1
Borrowed and Foreign Words

Like living things, language continues to grow and change. New words and expressions continually come into the English language from other cultures. This chart shows examples of such **borrowed and foreign words.**

English word	Borrowed from	Meaning
collage	French	piece of art made by pasting items together
wander	German	to roam
soprano	Italian	the highest singing voice
pinto	Spanish	a spotted horse
kayak	Inuit	a flat boat
okra	African	a plant with edible pods

A. DIRECTIONS: *Use a dictionary to find the original source of each of these borrowed and foreign words. Add the source and the meaning to the chart.*

English word	Borrowed from	Meaning
1. yoga		
2. bagel		
3. maelstrom		
4. skunk		
5. magenta		
6. pronto		
7. banjo		
8. avalanche		

Name _____ Date _____

Unit 5 Vocabulary Workshop—2
Borrowed and Foreign Words

The English language also contains many words that were borrowed from another source—people's names. Such words are called **eponymous words.** For example, the word maverick means "a person who takes an independent stand and does not follow the rules or practices of others." This eponymous word comes from the name of Sam Maverick (1803-1870), a Texas rancher who, unlike his neighbors, did not brand his cattle.

B. DIRECTIONS: *Use a dictionary to find the source of each of the following eponymous words. Add the source and the meaning to the chart.*

English word	Borrowed from the name of	Meaning
1. zinnia		
2. boycott		
3. quisling		
4. adonis		
5. curie		
6. madeleine		
7. einsteinium		
8. charlotte		
9. macadam		
10. pasteurize		

Name _____ Date _____

Evaluating Media Messages

After choosing your commercial, fill out the following chart to evaluate the effects and techniques of what you see.

Title of commercial: _____

What are some of the images presented in the commercial?
What is the message behind them?
What mood is created by the sound effects or music?
What techniques are used to persuade you to agree with this message?
How would you rate the credibility of this message?

Unit 5: Drama
Benchmark Test 10

MULTIPLE CHOICE

Reading Skill: Summarize *Read the selection. Then, answer the questions that follow.*

[1] Lydia Kamakameha was born in 1838 into a high-ranking family in Hawaii. In her twenties, she married the son of a Boston sea captain. When Lydia's brother died in 1891, Lydia became queen of Hawaii and was given the royal name Queen Liliuokalani. As queen, she strongly favored Hawaii's independence and actively fought against annexation of her beloved islands by the United States.

[2] Nonnative Hawaiians with businesses in the islands opposed the queen because she refused to recognize special rights and privileges for their businesses. In 1893, Liliuokalani was dethroned as a result of her refusal and temporarily put under house arrest. After her public life, Liliuokalani wrote songs and books about Hawaii. She composed "Aloha Oe," one of the best-known Hawaiian songs. Queen Liliuokalani died in 1917, in Honolulu, Hawaii.

1. Which of the following is the least important detail in paragraph 1?
   A. Lydia was given the name Liliuokalani.
   B. Lydia's husband was the son of a sea captain.
   C. The queen favored Hawaii's independence.
   D. Liliuokalani did not want Hawaii annexed to the United States.

2. Which of the following would be important in summarizing the selection?
   A. knowing something about the author
   B. analyzing an author's purpose
   C. identifying important ideas in the selection
   D. relating what you know to the selection

3. Which of these is the best summary of paragraph 1?
   A. Lydia Kamakameha was born into a high-ranking family and married the son of a sea captain in her twenties.
   B. As Queen Liliuokalani, the former Lydia Kamakameha fought for Hawaiian independence.
   C. Lydia Kamakameha was born in 1838 and became queen when her brother died, in 1891.
   D. When she succeeded her brother as ruler of Hawaii, Liliuokalani fought to keep Hawaii independent.

4. Which information from paragraph 2 would you include in a summary of the selection?
   A. The queen was dethroned in 1893.
   B. The queen was put under house arrest.
   C. The queen died in Honolulu, Hawaii.
   D. "Aloha Oe" is a well-known song.

5. Which of the following is the best summary of paragraph 2?
   A. Nonnative Hawaiians wanted to keep special rights and privileges, but the queen opposed them.
   B. Dethroned in 1893 for opposing rights for nonnative businesses, the queen retired to write until her death, in 1917.
   C. After being deposed, the queen wrote books and songs about Hawaii, one of which became well known.
   D. Some business owners opposed the queen and were able to get her dethroned, in 1893.

Reading Skill: Identify Bias and Stereotyping *Read the selection. Then, answer the questions that follow.*

While television can be entertaining and educational, it also has a dark side, especially for children. On average, children spend nearly 4 hours a day watching television. The harmful effects of television viewing far outweigh any benefits.

Doing poorly in school is one negative effect of too much television. One study found that children who watch 10 hours or more of TV each week are less skilled at reading and less successful in school. These children watch television instead of reading, doing homework, pursing hobbies, and getting enough sleep. In fact, watching too much television can lead to sleep disorders in children and teenagers. And this is not the only health problem TV viewing can cause. Children who are watching television are not getting any exercise. In addition, they are bombarded by commercials that unethical sponsors use to tempt them with unhealthy snack foods and drinks. No wonder children who watch more television are more likely to be overweight. The Centers for Disease Control and Prevention have found that the rate of obesity was highest among children who watched 4 or more hours of TV a day, and lowest among children watching an hour or less a day.

Parents can make a difference. They can limit television watching to no more than 1–2 hours a day. They can watch public television, rent quality videos, or record programs and leave out the commercials. They can encourage their children to explore other options such as playing, reading, participating in sports, or learning a hobby. And, most important of all, they can set a good example.

6. Which of the following phrases shows a bias on the part of the author?
   A. especially for children
   B. unethical sponsors
   C. altered sleep patterns
   D. explore other options

7. Which claim from the selection is least supported by factual evidence?
   A. The harmful effects of television viewing far outweigh any benefits.
   B. Doing poorly in school is one negative effect of too much television.
   C. And this is not the only health problem TV viewing can cause.
   D. No wonder children who watch more television are more likely to be overweight.

8. Which of the following does the author use to support the argument that parents can make a difference?
   A. facts and figures
   B. emotional appeals
   C. stereotypes
   D. examples

Literary Analysis: Characters' Motives *Read the selection. Then, answer the questions that follow.*

In a small town there lived a poor shoemaker and his daughter, Sophia. One day, as the shoemaker approached the town with a wagonload of new shoes, a wealthy merchant stopped him and asked, "How much for everything?" The shoemaker named a fair price, which the merchant accepted. Then, the merchant climbed in the wagon and claimed it, saying, "You agreed to sell me 'everything,' didn't you? That includes your wagon and horse."

When Sophia heard about this, she had an idea. The next day, she loaded some shoes in a wheelbarrow and went to town. When the merchant saw her, he asked, "How much for everything?" He reached into his pocket and produced three copper pieces. Sophia said she would take everything in his hand. When the merchant agreed, Sophia then told him that "everything" included the merchant's fine ring on his hand. Sophia offered to trade the ring for her father's wagon and horse. Realizing that he'd been tricked, the merchant agreed. And so Sophia returned home with her father's horse and wagon, and three copper pieces as well.

9. Which of the following best defines *characters' motives*?
   A. persons or animals in a literary work
   B. the reasons for characters' actions
   C. the process of creating characters
   D. the traits of characters

10. Which word best states the main motive of the merchant in this story?
   A. power
   B. greed
   C. jealousy
   D. anger

11. Why does Sophia go to town?
   A. She wants to give the merchant his money back.
   B. She wants to buy goods from the merchant.
   C. She wants to sell more shoes in the market.
   D. She wants to get her father's wagon and horse back.

12. What is the merchant's reason for giving Sophia the horse and wagon?
   A. He feels guilty for tricking her father.
   B. Sophia has paid him a fair price.
   C. He wants to keep his ring.
   D. He wants to make a fair trade.

Literary Analysis: Comparing Dramatic Speeches *Read the selections. Then, answer the questions that follow.*

Speech 1:

When I look at our community library, I realize what people can accomplish by working together. I'm remembering how Ms. Hannah and Mr. Floyd suspended their decades-long feud to work together to raise money for the library. I am reminded of times when my family and friends encouraged me to complete a different task. By ourselves, we can't do much; together, we're more powerful than we imagine.

Speech 2:

Marcus. The thing is, we've got to look out for ourselves. You just can't depend on others.

Aisha. Why do you say that?

Marcus. Because it's true. People will always let you down.

Aisha. I disagree. You're being unfair.

Marcus. I'm being realistic. For instance, when I asked Jeff to help me with a science project, he was too busy. When Tim agreed to be my jogging partner, he broke his ankle.

13. Which of the following best describes Speech 1?
   A. dialogue
   B. monologue
   C. narration
   D. dialect

14. Which of the following is a characteristic of a dramatic speech?
    A. It is a long speech by a main character.
    B. It moves the action of a story forward.
    C. It usually involves two characters.
    D. It resolves a conflict in a drama.

15. Which of the following best describes the speaker in Speech 1?
    A. humble and admiring of others
    B. full of self-importance
    C. too eager to give others credit
    D. ambitious and self-confident

16. Which of the following best describes Marcus in Speech 2?
    A. eager to find fault in others
    B. unwilling to admit mistakes
    C. practical and sensible
    D. lacking faith in others

Vocabulary: Roots

17. How does the meaning of the word *insist* reflect the meaning of the root *-sist-*?
    A. When you insist on something, you take and maintain a stand.
    B. When you insist on something, you give your opinion.
    C. When you insist on something, you can offend others.
    D. When you insist on something, you feel strongly about it.

18. Using your knowledge of the root *-sist-*, what does the word *resist* mean in the following sentence?

    She will resist the plan to close the library.

    A. agree to
    B. stand up against
    C. help put together
    D. take a look at

19. Based on your knowledge of the root *-sist-*, what is the function of your *assistant*?
    A. to lead you
    B. to protect you
    C. to teach you
    D. to help you

20. Using your knowledge of the root *-sist-*, what does the word *subsist* mean in the following sentence?

    The lost hiker found it difficult to subsist in the wilderness.

    A. have fun
    B. stay alive
    C. find nourishment
    D. calm down

21. What is the meaning of *scientific* in the following sentence?

    Ms. Nguyen used a scientific approach to finding the cause of the leak.

    A. one who uses the methods of science
    B. the result of technology
    C. relating to science
    D. the product of factual knowledge

22. What is the meaning of *criticize* in the following sentence?

    Emil squinted thoughtfully at the artwork, and then began to criticize its every aspect.

    A. a type of examination
    B. to make a judgment
    C. relating to an object's worth
    D. a state of being judged

23. What is the meaning of *poetic* in the following sentence?

At dinner, Carson delivered a poetic tribute to his father's tuna casserole.

A. one who writes verse
B. resembling a poet
C. to create a poem
D. relating to poetry

24. What is the meaning of *civilize* in the following sentence?

Huck Finn feared that his aunt would try to civilize him.

A. to make better behaved
B. pertaining to courtesy
C. the result of civil action
D. the state of being improved

Grammar: Sentence Functions and End Marks

25. Which of the following sentences is a command?
A. Do you enjoy gospel music?
B. Please lock the door when you leave.
C. What an amazing sunset!
D. Cattle drives were long and difficult.

26. Which category best describes the following sentence?

Can kangaroos walk on all four legs?

A. declarative
B. interrogative
C. imperative
D. exclamatory

27. Which of the following sentences uses correct end punctuation?
A. Give me your unwanted shoes?
B. Did you see the glassblower.
C. Run for your life.
D. Those waves are awesome!

Grammar: Revising for Subject-Verb Agreement of Compound Subjects

28. What is the best way to correct the following sentence?

Swimming and baseball is my favorite sports.

A. Change *and* to *or.*
B. Change *is* to *were.*
C. Change *is* to *are.*
D. Change *sports* to *sport.*

29. Which sentence has correct subject-verb agreement?
A. A train or a bus provide a hands-free way to travel.
B. Taking deep breaths or going for a walk helps the body relax.
C. Either Sally or Jessica know how to operate this machine.
D. Cities or states pays for local public libraries.

30. In which sentence do the subjects and verb agree?
A. Both cats and dogs sometimes gets fleas.
B. Neither Philip nor Angie wants to cancel the show.
C. Automobiles and factories creates smog.
D. Smoke or steam are rising from the neighbor's house.

Spelling: Plurals

31. Which sentence has the correct plural form of *journey*?

    A. The explorers kept notes on their many journies.

    B. How many journeyes did Columbus make to America?

    C. The settlers' journeys west took many months.

    D. Kellerman became lost on the first of several journys to Africa.

32. Which sentence has the correct plural form of *goose*?

    A. Nine geese flew in formation overhead.

    B. E. B. White kept several gooses.

    C. The goose were loud and ill-mannered.

    D. I startled two geeses near the pond.

33. Which sentence has the correct plural form of *waltz*?

    A. Johann Strauss wrote many waltzs.

    B. The dancers performed three waltzes.

    C. I cannot name many waltzies.

    D. Viennese waltzses are light and airy.

ESSAY

Writing

34. Suppose that the mayor of your town has asked you to write a report on conditions in your neighborhood. In particular, the mayor would like to know your recommendations for changes that would improve the neighborhood. On a separate sheet of paper, write a paragraph in which you describe (1) how you will gather information for the report; (2) how you will organize the report; and (3) two or more recommendations for changes that you might include.

35. Think of at least four topics for a cause-and-effect essay. On a separate sheet of paper, jot down the topics. Then, choose the one topic that most interests you. Write a sentence and tell why the topic is interesting to you. Finally, list at least three questions you hope to answer in your essay.

36. Think of an occurrence in nature that interests you. For example, you might be interested in finding out more about lightning or hibernation. Imagine that you are preparing to write a cause-and-effect essay on this occurrence. In order to narrow your topic, draw a topic web on a separate sheet of paper. First, draw a circle in the center of your page. Then, write the topic inside the circle. Next, write at least four connected ideas or questions inside new circles around your topic. Draw lines connecting these ideas to the main topic.

Vocabulary in Context

Identify the answer choice that best completes the statement.

1. Take off your wet bathing suit, and put on your clothes in the_____ .
   A. patio
   B. location
   C. courtyard
   D. bathhouse

2. After finishing my bath, I_____ the tub.
   A. drained
   B. sucked
   C. capped
   D. relaxed

3. Tomorrow we will leave the island and return to the_____ .
   A. site
   B. landscape
   C. mainland
   D. household

4. When you hike in the woods, be on the lookout for sharp_____ .
   A. gems
   B. pears
   C. peaks
   D. thistles

5. After pulling out the weeds, I noticed a_____ on my arm.
   A. evidence
   B. rash
   C. pang
   D. cleft

6. Like a fox, she was very_____ .
   A. glittering
   B. charming
   C. cunning
   D. proclaimed

7. The mayor will be choosing and_____ a new chief of police.
   A. appropriating
   B. assembling
   C. appointing
   D. attending

8. As for the future, the following are my_____ .
   A. creations
   B. predictions
   C. illustrations
   D. dispositions

9. I guess that area of land is_____ 100 acres.
   A. exhibited
   B. mightily
   C. absolutely
   D. approximately

10. In a small pond, we set the toy boat_____ .
    A. onward
    B. afloat
    C. aloft
    D. afar

11. After a long winter, it is nice to see the flowers_____ .
    A. overcome
    B. wavering
    C. ornament
    D. blossoming

12. The eagles in the museum's display had sharp_____ .
    A. caw
    B. croon
    C. talons
    D. utensils

13. In ancient Rome, people often traveled in_____ .
    A. mobiles
    B. chariots
    C. boxcars
    D. stagecoaches

14. He ruled the kingdom as its_____ .
    A. corpse
    B. heiress
    C. monarch
    D. historian

15. I was so thirsty that even the warm water_____ my thirst.
   A. quenched
   B. wavered
   C. imprisoned
   D. accomplished

16. The old building had fallen and all that remained was a pile of_____ .
   A. shrines
   B. pyramids
   C. fragments
   D. ornaments

17. When our parrot died, we gave it a proper_____ .
   A. reign
   B. realm
   C. burial
   D. heiress

18. This is my house, or as I often say, my humble_____ .
   A. abode
   B. darkroom
   C. waterways
   D. underworld

19. I certainly am happy you invited me; in fact, I am_____ glad.
   A. vainly
   B. doubly
   C. refrain
   D. glamorously

20. The sky was darkened from the hundreds of_____ flying overhead.
   A. seers
   B. ostrich
   C. varmints
   D. blackbirds

Diagnostic Tests and Vocabulary in Context
Use and Interpretation

The Diagnostic Tests and Vocabulary in Context were developed to assist teachers in making the most appropriate assignment of *Prentice Hall Literature* program selections to students. The purpose of these assessments is to indicate the degree of difficulty that students are likely to have in reading/comprehending the selections presented in the *following* unit of instruction. Tests are provided at six separate times in each in each grade level—a *Diagnostic Test* (to be used prior to beginning the year's instruction) and a *Vocabulary in Context,* the final segment of the Benchmark Test appearing at the end of each of the first five units of instruction. Note that the tests are intended for use not as summative assessments for the prior unit, but as guidance for assigning literature selections in the upcoming unit of instruction.

The structure of all Diagnostic Tests and Vocabulary in Context in this series is the same. All test items are four-option, multiple-choice items. The format is established to assess a student's ability to construct sufficient meaning from the context sentence to choose the only provided word that fits both the semantics (meaning) and syntax (structure) of the context sentence. All words in the context sentences are chosen to be "below-level" words that students reading at this grade level should know. All answer choices fit *either* the meaning or structure of the context sentence, but only the correct choice fits *both* semantics and syntax. All answer choices—both correct answers and incorrect options—are key words chosen from specifically taught words that will occur in the subsequent unit of program instruction. This careful restriction of the assessed words permits a sound diagnosis of students' current reading achievement and prediction of the most appropriate level of readings to assign in the upcoming unit of instruction.

The assessment of vocabulary in context skill has consistently been shown in reading research studies to correlate very highly with "reading comprehension." This is not surprising as the format essentially assesses comprehension, albeit in sentence-length "chunks." Decades of research demonstrate that vocabulary assessment provides a strong, reliable prediction of comprehension achievement—the purpose of these tests. Further, because this format demands very little testing time, these diagnoses can be made efficiently, permitting teachers to move forward with critical instructional tasks rather than devoting excessive time to assessment.

It is important to stress that while the Diagnostic and Vocabulary in Context were carefully developed and will yield sound assignment decisions, they were designed to *reinforce,* not supplant, teacher judgment as to the most appropriate instructional placement for individual students. Teacher judgment should always prevail in making placement—or indeed other important instructional—decisions concerning students.

Diagnostic Tests and Vocabulary in Context Branching Suggestions

These tests are designed to provide maximum flexibility for teachers. Your *Unit Resources* books contain the 40-question **Diagnostic Test** and 20-question **Vocabulary in Context** tests. At *PHLitOnline,* you can access the Diagnostic Test and complete 40-question Vocabulary in Context tests. Procedures for administering the tests are described below. Choose the procedure based on the time you wish to devote to the activity and your comfort with the assignment decisions relative to the individual students. Remember that your judgment of a student's reading level should always take precedence over the results of a single written test.

Feel free to use different procedures at different times of the year. For example, for early units, you may wish to be more confident in the assignments you make—thus, using the "two-stage" process below. Later, you may choose the quicker diagnosis, confirming the results with your observations of the students' performance built up throughout the year.

The **Diagnostic Test** is composed of a single 40-item assessment. Based on the results of this assessment, make the following assignment of students to the reading selections in Unit 1:

Diagnostic Test Score	Selection to Use
If the student's score is 0–25	more accessible
If the student's score is 26–40	more challenging

Outlined below are the three basic options for administering **Vocabulary in Context** and basing selection assignments on the results of these assessments.

1. For a one-stage, quicker diagnosis using the *20-item* test in the *Unit Resources:*

Vocabulary in Context Test Score	Selection to Use
If the student's score is 0–13	more accessible
If the student's score is 14–20	more challenging

2. If you wish to confirm your assignment decisions with a *two-stage* diagnosis:

Stage 1: Administer the 20-item test in the *Unit Resources*	
Vocabulary in Context Test Score	Selection to Use
If the student's score is 0–9	more accessible
If the student's score is 10–15	(Go to Stage 2.)
If the student's score is 16–20	more challenging

Stage 2: Administer items 21–40 from *PHLitOnline*	
Vocabulary in Context Test Score	Selection to Use
If the student's score is 0–12	more accessible
If the student's score is 13–20	more challenging

3. If you base your assignment decisions on the full 40-item **Vocabulary in Context** from *PHLitOnline:*

Vocabulary in Context Test Score	Selection to Use
If the student's score is 0–25	more accessible
If the student's score is 26–40	more challenging

Name _____ Date _____

Grade 7—Benchmark Test 9
Interpretation Guide

For remediation of specific skills, you may assign students the relevant Reading Kit Practice and Assess pages indicated in the far-right column of this chart. You will find rubrics for evaluating writing samples in the last section of your Professional Development Guidebook.

Skill Objective	Test Items	Number Correct	Reading Kit
Reading Skill			
Setting a Purpose	1, 2, 3, 4, 5, 6, 7		pp. 200, 201
Analyze the Author's Perspective	8, 9, 10		pp. 202, 203
Literary Analysis			
Dialogue	11, 12, 13		pp. 204, 205
Stage Directions	14, 15, 16		pp. 206, 207
Comparing characters	17, 18, 19		pp. 208, 209
Vocabulary			
Roots and Prefixes -grat-, inter-	20, 21, 22, 23, 24, 25		pp. 210, 211
Grammar			
Interjections	26, 27, 28		pp. 212, 213
Double Negatives	29, 30, 31		pp. 214, 215
Common Usage Problems	32, 33		pp. 216, 217
Writing			
Letter	34	Use rubric	pp. 218, 219
Tribute	35	Use rubric	pp. 220, 221
Multimedia Report	36	Use rubric	pp. 222, 223

Grade 7—Benchmark Test 10
Interpretation Guide

For remediation of specific skills, you may assign students the relevant Reading Kit Practice and Assess pages indicated in the far-right column of this chart. You will find rubrics for evaluating writing samples in the last section of your Professional Development Guidebook.

Skill Objective	Test Items	Number Correct	Reading Kit
Reading Skill			
Summary	1, 2, 3, 4, 5		pp. 224, 225
Identify Bias and Stereotyping	6, 7, 8		pp. 226, 227
Literary Analysis			
Character's Motives	9, 10, 11, 12		pp. 228, 229
Dramatic Speeches	13, 14, 15, 16		pp. 230, 231
Vocabulary			
Roots -*sist*-	17, 18, 19, 20, 21, 22, 23, 24		pp. 232, 233
Grammar			
Sentence Functions and End marks	25, 26, 27		pp. 234, 235
Subject-Verb Agreement with Compound Subjects	28, 29, 30		pp. 236, 237
Spelling			
Plurals	31, 32, 33		pp. 238, 239
Writing			
Report	34	Use rubric	pp. 240, 241
Cause-and-Effect Essay	35, 36	Use rubric	pp. 242, 243

ANSWERS

Big Question Vocabulary—1, p. 1

A. 1. synonym: be thankful; antonym: be ungrateful
2. synonym: theory; antonym: proof
3. synonym: prejudice; antonym: fairness
4. synonym: characterize; antonym: distort
5. synonym: uncover; antonym: hide

B. Stories will vary, but should reflect the assignment and contain all five vocabulary words.

Big Question Vocabulary—2, p. 2

A. 1. ignore
2. perspective
3. appearance
4. focus
5. identify

B. Sentences may vary. Possible responses are shown.
1. False; A person's appearance is the way he or she looks to others.
2. False; If the fire alarm goes off, the best course of action is to head for an exit quickly.
3. False; To board an airplane, you must carry a photo I.D. in order to identify yourself.
4. False; activities that require you to focus carefully include studying and solving problems.
5. True

Big Question Vocabulary—3, p. 3

Answers will vary. Possible responses are shown.

Mario: It's hard to form an image of this man in my mind. Describe some of his characteristics.

Heidi: Had you ever seen him before? If not, your perception of him as a spooky magician seems accurate!

Ramon: It's easy to see why you almost fainted. That reaction would certainly reflect your shock!

from Dragonwings by Laurence Yep

Vocabulary Warm-up Exercises, p. 8

A. 1. contraption
2. demonstration
3. haul
4. audience
5. serious
6. repeat
7. steep
8. flight

B. Sample Answers
1. Egg yolks and egg whites might be *separated* so that the egg whites could be beaten for a special recipe.
2. If I *expected* to win a special award, I might prepare an acceptance speech.

3. Two *machines* I might use at home would be a vacuum cleaner and a garbage disposal.
4. An *immigration* officer makes sure that people coming into the United States have permission to do so.
5. If I dropped my clothes off at a *laundry*, I would want them to be washed and ironed or folded.
6. To earn money, *merchants* sell or trade things.
7. If Alex says he will *probably* go to a party, there is a good chance he will be there, but it is not certain.
8. The last time I got sick, it took me three days to *recover*.

Reading Warm-up A, p. 9

Sample Answers

1. Besides you and the Wrights, four men and a boy are there to witness this demonstration. The last time I was part of an *audience*, I saw a basketball game.
2. see if they will actually fly this time, *witness*; The *demonstration* proved that the kite could fly quite high.
3. (aeroplane); Nobody had ever seen such a strange *contraption*.
4. flat; I would rather climb a *steep* hill because it is more of a challenge.
5. (to the sand bar at Kitty Hawk); The last time I had to *haul* something heavy from one place to another was when I moved my dresser to the other side of my room.
6. 12 seconds; 120 feet; *Flight* means "relating to the act or manner of flying."
7. (the plane needs major repairs); I hurt my wrist playing volleyball, but the injury was not *serious*.
8. the experiment; *Repeat* means "to do over again."

Reading Warm-up B, p. 10

Sample Answers

1. the war; If I were trying to *recover* from a disappointment, I might try to stay busy with things that would distract me.
2. (to work for very little pay); I *expected* Marie to join me for lunch on Wednesday.
3. they were welcomed at first; *Immigration* means "coming to a foreign country to live there."
4. (they worked hard), (they kept to themselves); This is *most likely* because they worked hard and kept to themselves.
5. their families; Jennie *separated* the blue beads from the yellow beads.
6. (people who didn't want to wash and iron their own clothes); I might find shirts, slacks, and other things that need washing and ironing at a *laundry*.
7. produce manufactured goods; *Machines* are "mechanical devices or equipment."
8. (shopkeepers and traders); The *merchants* on Sutter Street sell a variety of products.

Laurence Yep

Listening and Viewing, p. 11

Sample answers and guidelines for evaluation:

Segment 1. Laurence Yep read science-fiction stories because the characters were taken to different worlds and had to learn new customs and languages. Students should provide a reasonable explanation for their reaction to Yep's interest in science fiction. Most likely, they will say that they are not surprised because science fiction is exciting, or they may draw a connection between Yep's background as a Chinese American growing up in two cultures and the experiences of characters in science fiction, who often encounter cultures other than their own.

Segment 2. Yep points out that novels contain more detail than dramas and build a complete world for the reader. Dramas sketch the background and provide a strong physical and emotional presence. Students should provide a reasonable explanation for their choice of the more difficult genre to write. They may suggest that a drama would be more difficult because the story must be told largely through dialogue. Alternatively, they may say that it would be more difficult to write a novel because it is so long that it might easily become boring.

Segment 3. Yep continuously rewrites to add details and layers to his original story. Students may suggest that, like Yep, they would do research to gather background material, set a schedule to be productive, or rewrite to add details and "layers."

Segment 4. Yep believes that books can open doors. They can take readers to new places, give them new experiences, and show them that they are not alone.

Unit 5: Learning About Drama, p. 12

A. 1. It is a kitchen at 7 A.M. There is a table, at least one chair, and a door.

2. The props are a newspaper and a book bag.

3. "almost shouting" *or* "patiently"

4. "rushes in" *or* "getting up from the table"

5. It is dialogue, a conversation between two characters. There are no long speeches.

6. Students will probably say that it seems to be from a comedy because it involves normal characters, and one has made a humorous mistake.

from **Dragonwings** by Laurence Yep

Model Selection: Drama, p. 13

A. 1. The setting is Piedmont, outside a stable.

2. Moon Shadow is most likely using paper and a pen or pencil.

3. Guidelines for evaluation: Sound effects include a cough as the motor starts, the roar as the propellers turn, the roar of the plane in flight, and a gong at the end of the scene.

4. The speech is a monologue. It is a long speech involving only a single character, and it reveals the character's thoughts.

5. Sample answer: The main character is Moon Shadow. He appears at the beginning of the scene and again at the end. The events seem to be told from his point of view, and he reveals his thoughts in a monologue.

B. Students should recognize that the climax occurs when the airplane takes off. They should recognize that Windrider realizes that when he was flying, Moon Shadow seemed to be disappearing from his life; he realizes that he must give up flying and dedicate himself to his family. Although Moon Shadow is the main character, his insights in response to the flight are not clearly articulated. Students should note that by appearing as an adult in the cap his father gives him after the failed flight and by referring to never-forgotten dreams, he shows that in some way his father's dream of flying has had an important influence on his life.

Open-Book Test, p. 14

Short Answer

1. It is a monologue because only one person is speaking. A dialogue would be a conversation between or among characters.

   Difficulty: *Easy* **Objective:** *Literary Analysis*

2. Stage directions describe scenery and tell how characters should move and how they should speak. They can also describe sound effects.

   Difficulty: *Average* **Objective:** *Literary Analysis*

3. The key is a prop. Actors use props to make their actions look believable.

   Difficulty: *Average* **Objective:** *Literary Analysis*

4. Screenplay: a script for a film; may include camera angles

   Teleplay: written to be performed on television; may include camera angles

   Radio Play: written to be performed on radio broadcasts; includes sound effects

   Students should give the title of a novel and, using the elements of each, give an explanation why it would or would not make a good screenplay, teleplay, or radio play.

   Difficulty: *Average* **Objective:** *Literary Analysis*

5. It tells the reader where and when the scene takes place. It is a stage direction.

   Difficulty: *Easy* **Objective:** *Literary Analysis*

6. Uncle Bright Star wants to get everyone to work hard and to work at the same rhythmic pace.

   Difficulty: *Average* **Objective:** *Interpretation*

7. The playwright uses stage directions to indicate that the audience should hear or imagine the flight of the plane.

   Difficulty: *Challenging* **Objective:** *Literary Analysis*

8. It is called a flight ballet, representing the flight of the airplane.

Unit 5 Resources: Drama

Difficulty: *Easy*   **Objective:** *Interpretation*

9. Windrider asks Moon Shadow if he would like to send for his mother, suggesting that she will come from China.

Difficulty: *Average*   **Objective:** *Interpretation*

10. Moon Shadow; he is the narrator and action revolves around him.

Difficulty: *Challenging*   **Objective:** *Interpretation*

Essay

11. Students should recognize that Windrider is a dreamer. The monologue suggests that he now has put his responsibilities as a father ahead of his dreams. His decision to work in the laundry and bring Moon Shadow's mother from China supports this analysis.

Difficulty: *Easy*   **Objective:** *Essay*

12. Students should recognize that the playwright wants the cap to indicate the relationship between father and son. The playwright may also be asking the audience to associate the cap with the flight of the airplane and the father's dream. Students should note that when Moon Shadow wears the cap at the end of the scene, it shows that he respects and admires his father.

Difficulty: *Average*   **Objective:** *Essay*

13. Students should recognize that the ending allows the audience to know that Windrider never flies again, though he always dreams of flying. They might note that for Moon Shadow, the important thing was that they never forgot their flight and the dream they shared. Students may suggest that their shared memory probably helped keep them close later in life.

Difficulty: *Challenging*   **Objective:** *Essay*

14. Students should note that Windrider says he saw Moon Shadow "getting smaller" and disappearing "from my life." They may feel that this suggests Windrider is really seeing his son and recognizing Moon Shadow's importance in his life. It results in his changing his plans for the future.

Difficulty: *Average*   **Objective:** *Essay*

Oral Response

15. Oral responses should be clear, well organized, and well supported by appropriate examples from the selection.

Difficulty: *Average*   **Objective:** *Oral Interpretation*

Selection Test A, p. 17

Learning About Drama

1. ANS: C	DIF: Easy	OBJ: Literary Analysis
2. ANS: C	DIF: Easy	OBJ: Literary Analysis
3. ANS: B	DIF: Easy	OBJ: Literary Analysis
4. ANS: B	DIF: Easy	OBJ: Literary Analysis

5. ANS: D	DIF: Easy	OBJ: Literary Analysis
6. ANS: A	DIF: Easy	OBJ: Literary Analysis

Critical Reading

7. ANS: B	DIF: Easy	OBJ: Literary Analysis
8. ANS: D	DIF: Easy	OBJ: Comprehension
9. ANS: C	DIF: Easy	OBJ: Comprehension
10. ANS: A	DIF: Easy	OBJ: Comprehension
11. ANS: B	DIF: Easy	OBJ: Comprehension
12. ANS: D	DIF: Easy	OBJ: Comprehension
13. ANS: D	DIF: Easy	OBJ: Interpretation
14. ANS: C	DIF: Easy	OBJ: Literary Analysis
15. ANS: C	DIF: Easy	OBJ: Comprehension

Essay

16. Students should recognize that Windrider is a dreamer. The monologue suggests that until now he has put his dreams ahead of his responsibilities as a father and husband, but the flight in the airplane has changed him, and now, he says, he wishes to fulfill his responsibilities. Students may refer to his decision to work for Uncle Bright Star in the laundry and bring Moon Shadow's mother from China.

Difficulty: *Easy*

Objective: *Essay*

17. Students should express some understanding of the importance of the dream of flying to Moon Shadow, or they might tie the line to Moon Shadow's apparent respect for and admiration of his father.

Difficulty: *Easy*

Objective: *Essay*

18. Students should note that Windrider says he saw Moon Shadow "getting smaller" and disappearing "from my life." They may feel that this suggests that Windrider is really seeing his son and recognizing Moon Shadow's importance in his life. It results in his changing his plans for the future.

Difficulty: *Average*

Objective: *Essay*

Selection Test B, p. 20

Learning About Drama

1. ANS: C	DIF: Average	OBJ: Literary Analysis
2. ANS: A	DIF: Average	OBJ: Literary Analysis
3. ANS: D	DIF: Challenging	OBJ: Literary Analysis
4. ANS: C	DIF: Challenging	OBJ: Literary Analysis
5. ANS: D	DIF: Challenging	OBJ: Literary Analysis
6. ANS: C	DIF: Average	OBJ: Literary Analysis

Critical Reading

7. ANS: A	DIF: Average	OBJ: Comprehension
8. ANS: C	DIF: Average	OBJ: Comprehension
9. ANS: B	DIF: Average	OBJ: Comprehension
10. ANS: D	DIF: Average	OBJ: Comprehension
11. ANS: C	DIF: Challenging	OBJ: Literary Analysis
12. ANS: B	DIF: Average	OBJ: Interpretation
13. ANS: D	DIF: Average	OBJ: Interpretation
14. ANS: A	DIF: Average	OBJ: Interpretation
15. ANS: C	DIF: Challenging	OBJ: Comprehension
16. ANS: B	DIF: Average	OBJ: Comprehension
17. ANS: A	DIF: Average	OBJ: Interpretation
18. ANS: D	DIF: Average	OBJ: Comprehension
19. ANS: D	DIF: Challenging	OBJ: Interpretation

Essay

20. Students should recognize that the cap in some way symbolizes the relationship between the father and his son. They may also associate it with the flight of the airplane or with the father's decision to give up flying, go to work for Uncle, and bring his wife from China. They should recognize that Moon Shadow wears the cap at the end of the scene, when he appears as an adult, to show that he respects and admires his father.

Difficulty: *Average*

Objective: *Essay*

21. Students should recognize that the ending provides a resolution: It allows the audience to know that Windrider never flies again, though he always dreamed of flying. They might also note that by giving Moon Shadow the final lines, the playwright brings the focus back to him, reminding the audience that he is the main character of the play.

Difficulty: *Average*

Objective: *Essay*

22. Students should note that Windrider says he saw Moon Shadow "getting smaller" and disappearing "from my life." This may suggest that Windrider is really seeing his son and recognizing Moon Shadow's importance in his life. It results in his changing his plans for the future.

Difficulty: *Average*

Objective: *Essay*

A Christmas Carol: Scrooge and Marley, *Act I*,
by Israel Horovitz

Vocabulary Warm-up Exercises, p. 24

A.
1. gold
2. perfection
3. miser
4. shrivels
5. penance
6. lustrous
7. resolute
8. replenish

B. Sample Answers
1. *establishments/businesses;* Many businesses flourish in the downtown area.
2. *welfare/well-being;* After the hurricane hit, the well-being of the residents was a big concern.
3. *impropriety/misbehavior;* So impolite was the audience's misbehavior that they talked during the performance.
4. *bleak/cold;* The cold winter landscape did not look inviting.
5. *grindstone/millstone;* The team worked as hard as mules pulling a millstone.
6. *surviving/still-living;* The still-living family members gathered for a reunion.
7. *neglected/ignored;* The ignored needs of the less fortunate were not being met.

Reading Warm-up A, p. 25

Sample Answers
1. (hoarded all his valuables); A *miser* does not like to share his or her belongings with others.
2. shiny, yellow; Things made of *gold* might include coins or jewelry.
3. (his supply of gold); *Replenish* means "to make full again by supplying a new stock."
4. the brilliant, lustrous metal; *Perfection* to me is a beautifully written poem or a delicious ice cream sundae.
5. (brilliant); The *lustrous* sunshine made everything glow in its yellow light.
6. without food and drink, he could not live; *Shrivels* means "wrinkles or becomes withered."
7. determined; *Resolute* means "unwavering or determined."
8. (his greed); He wanted to do something to make up for his mistaken behavior in being a greedy miser.

Reading Warm-up B, p. 26

Sample Answers
1. hopeless; Some other things that might be *bleak* are cold, cloudy weather or the feeling people might have when coping with the aftermath of a hurricane that has caused much damage.
2. (boarding schools); The agency set up many *establishments* to help meet the needs of the voters.
3. (if one or both parents had died); *Surviving* means "still living or existing."
4. Children were often mangled by machinery. The shops were dismal, dirty places to work. The children toiled for long hours. They were powerless to rebel against these terrible conditions.; *Welfare* is "well-being."

5. dirty places to work; The *dismal* cabin was dark and dank.
6. (As a result of working long hours); "Noses to the grindstone" means "to always be working very hard." The expression comes from a millstone, also called a grindstone, which is continuously in operation.
7. if they were seen or heard around the family for whom they worked; *Impropriety* means "improper action or behavior."
8. (the basic needs of many children at work, school, and home); *Neglected* means "ignored or not properly cared for."

Writing About the Big Question, p. 27

A. 1. appreciate
2. define
3. reaction

B. Sample Answers
1. When my little brother cut his finger, I learned that I could be very calm in an emergency. When I babysat my cousin, I learned that I am good with babies.
2. About a year ago, my little brother cut his finger. My parents were out at the time. I **reacted** immediately, helping him clean and bandage the cut. Until this happened, I would have **assumed** that the **appearance** of all that blood would have upset me.

C. Sample Answer

The way we treat others reveals our character. Are you mean to your little brother? Don't be surprised if people notice how you act. These observers may decide that you are an unkind person. If you have a kind character, you should always treat other people with respect. Of course, nobody is perfect. It is making the effort that is important.

Reading: Preview a Text to Set a Purpose for Reading, p. 28

1. The play is set in offices, homes, and other locations in London.
2. The play takes place on Christmas Eve, Christmas Day, and the day after Christmas in 1843.
3. **Sample answers:** to learn about a subject, to learn what life was like in England in the mid-nineteenth century, to gain understanding, to find out what people thought and valued at that time
4. They are dressed for warmth in old-fashioned clothing.
5. **Sample answers:** to learn about a subject, to gain understanding
6. **Sample answer:** to be entertained

Literary Analysis: Dialogue, p. 29

1. Three characters are speaking: Scrooge, a "portly" man, and a "thin" man.
2. **Sample answer:** Scrooge is rude, ungenerous, unpleasant, self-serving, and arrogant.

3. **Sample answer:** Scrooge is harsh—he believes that people should accept the help offered by the establishments he supports. When the do-gooders suggest that many poor people cannot or will not go to those places, he suggests that those people deserve to die and that the society would be better off without them. The do-gooders apparently believe that the well-off are obliged to try to help the poor.
4. the thin man or the portly man

Vocabulary Builder, p. 30

A. Sample answers follow each yes or no designation:
1. No, he asked with great intensity; *implored* means "begged."
2. No, he disliked celebrations; *morose* means "gloomy."
3. No, the *destitute* are poverty-stricken.
4. No, he saw nothing; *void* means "emptiness."
5. Yes, he has; *conveyed* means "made known."
6. Yes, Fezziwig was a kind and generous employer.

B. 1. If you are *grateful,* someone may have done something nice for you.
2. *Gratitude* is a happy emotion.
3. You would value a *gratifying* friendship.

Enrichment: Social Services, p. 31

A. 1. Students might find the information they need at *www.fns.usda.gov/fsp/*. In a phone directory, they should look in the section that lists county or state agencies (sometimes called the blue pages), under Department of Social Services.
2. Students might begin their research at *www.salvationarmyusa.org* or look in a phone directory. They might also look in the yellow pages of a phone directory, under the heading "Social and Human Services."
3. Students should go to *www.redcross.org* or look up the agency in a phone directory.
4. Students might look in the blue or yellow pages of a phone directory or do an Internet search.
5. Students should provide information about an organization in their community that performs a social service. They should name the sponsor and describe its mission.

B. Students should describe the reaction they would expect Scrooge to have to one of the organizations they researched in part A of this activity. They should provide a well-reasoned explanation in support of their opinion.

Integrated Language Skills: Grammar, p. 32

A. Sample Answers
1. Oops, the cat spilled his food all over the floor.
2. Ouch! I dropped the hammer on my foot.
3. I worked for two hours in the hot sun. Whew!
4. Hmmm, I think this CD costs way too much.
5. Hey! Do not go near that downed electric wire.

B. Students should write three grammatically correct sentences, each containing an interjection and punctuated correctly.

Open-Book Test, p. 35

Short Answer

1. The amusing names might help a reader set a purpose of being entertained.
   Difficulty: *Average* **Objective:** *Reading*
2. Scrooge is a solitary, miserly man. Marley calls him "tightfisted" and "self-contained."
   Difficulty: *Easy* **Objective:** *Literary Analysis*
3. Cratchit is forgiving of Scrooge. His kind words about Scrooge in the face of Scrooge's rudeness show this.
   Difficulty: *Average* **Objective:** *Literary Analysis*
4. Scrooge trims his candle, looks under the sofa and table, and sees Marley's face in the pictures. These actions show that he is fearful and nervous.
   Difficulty: *Easy* **Objective:** *Interpretation*
5. He says that an undigested bit of food has affected his senses, as he tries to blame the vision on indigestion.
   Difficulty: *Challenging* **Objective:** *Interpretation*
6. Marley says he never did anything in his lifetime except make money, and now he is being punished for it.
   Difficulty: *Average* **Objective:** *Interpretation*
7. Fezziwig acts in a kind and generous way to his employees.
   Difficulty: *Average* **Objective:** *Vocabulary*
8. The audience learns how Scrooge grew to be so alone. By revealing more about Scrooge's character, the dialogue helps the plot move toward a point where Scrooge can change.
   Difficulty: *Challenging* **Objective:** *Literary Analysis*
9. The dialogue helps the reader hear how people spoke and it helps the audience know what was important to the people in mid-1800s England.
   Difficulty: *Challenging* **Objective:** *Literary Analysis*
10. Fan: reminds Scrooge that he once loved his sister
    Fezziwig: reminds Scrooge that it is possible to be a kind employer
    Woman: reminds Scrooge that he once loved and was loved
    Students might say that the Woman's reminder has the greatest impact because it is the last in the cumulative effect, the greatest loss to Scrooge, or the most emotionally laden.
    Difficulty: *Average* **Objective:** *Interpretation*

Essay

11. Students should recognize that Scrooge sees the holiday as a time when he loses money, revealing his cynical and cantankerous character. The nephew sees it as a time for goodwill and generosity, revealing his cheerful, generous attitude.
    Difficulty: *Easy* **Objective:** *Essay*
12. Students may say that they have more sympathy for Scrooge after understanding that as a child he was sent away by his father, treated harshly by a schoolmaster, and lost the woman he loved. Alternatively, they may say that they have less sympathy for him because he was loved by his sister, liked by Fezziwig and Dick Wilkins, and loved by a woman, but he chose to spend his life amassing wealth instead of enjoying friendship and love.
    Difficulty: *Average* **Objective:** *Essay*
13. Students should recognize that Marley is saying that he had misunderstood his business. He now realizes that he should have been working to help humanity. Students may justify this explanation by noting that Marley says that if people do not act in a positive way during their lifetimes, they are condemned to do so after they die.
    Difficulty: *Challenging* **Objective:** *Essay*
14. Students should point out that in Scene 1 Marley describes Scrooge as "tightfisted," "grasping," and "solitary." In Scene 3, however, Marley tells Scrooge that he has a chance and a hope of escaping his own fate, so he sees that Scrooge still has some humanity within him.
    Difficulty: *Average* **Objective:** *Essay*

Oral Response

15. Oral responses should be clear, well organized, and well supported by appropriate examples from the selection.
    Difficulty: *Average* **Objective:** *Oral Interpretation*

Selection Test A, p. 38

Critical Reading

1. ANS: C	DIF: Easy	OBJ: Reading
2. ANS: C	DIF: Easy	OBJ: Reading
3. ANS: B	DIF: Easy	OBJ: Reading
4. ANS: C	DIF: Easy	OBJ: Interpretation
5. ANS: A	DIF: Easy	OBJ: Literary Analysis
6. ANS: B	DIF: Easy	OBJ: Literary Analysis
7. ANS: D	DIF: Easy	OBJ: Comprehension
8. ANS: B	DIF: Easy	OBJ: Interpretation
9. ANS: D	DIF: Easy	OBJ: Interpretation
10. ANS: A	DIF: Easy	OBJ: Interpretation
11. ANS: A	DIF: Easy	OBJ: Literary Analysis

Vocabulary and Grammar

12. ANS: D	DIF: Easy	OBJ: Vocabulary
13. ANS: B	DIF: Easy	OBJ: Grammar

Essay

14. Guidelines for evaluation: Students should recognize the cynical and cantankerous attitude of Scrooge, who sees the holiday only as a time when he loses money, and the cheerful, generous attitude of the nephew, who sees the holiday as a time for goodwill and generosity.

    Difficulty: *Easy*
    Objective: *Essay*

15. Guidelines for evaluation: Students should recognize the similarities in the two men's lives. Scrooge may be influenced by Marley because they were equals—partners—at one time. In seeing Marley in chains, he has a sense of what awaits him if he does not reform.

    Difficulty: *Easy*
    Objective: *Essay*

16. Students might point out that in Scene 1, Marley describes Scrooge as "tightfisted," "grasping," and "solitary." In Scene 3, however, Marley tells Scrooge that he has a chance and a hope of escaping his own fate. This shows that Scrooge still has some humanity within him.

    Difficulty: *Average*
    Objective: *Essay*

Selection Test B, p. 41

Critical Reading

1. ANS: D	DIF: Average	OBJ: Reading
2. ANS: B	DIF: Average	OBJ: Reading
3. ANS: C	DIF: Average	OBJ: Reading
4. ANS: B	DIF: Average	OBJ: Comprehension
5. ANS: B	DIF: Challenging	OBJ: Literary Analysis
6. ANS: B	DIF: Average	OBJ: Literary Analysis
7. ANS: B	DIF: Challenging	OBJ: Interpretation
8. ANS: C	DIF: Challenging	OBJ: Interpretation
9. ANS: C	DIF: Challenging	OBJ: Interpretation
10. ANS: D	DIF: Challenging	OBJ: Comprehension
11. ANS: B	DIF: Average	OBJ: Literary Analysis
12. ANS: B	DIF: Challenging	OBJ: Literary Analysis

Vocabulary and Grammar

13. ANS: D	DIF: Average	OBJ: Vocabulary
14. ANS: A	DIF: Average	OBJ: Vocabulary
15. ANS: D	DIF: Average	OBJ: Grammar

Essay

16. Students may say that they have more sympathy for Scrooge now that they understand that as a child he was apparently sent away by his father and treated harshly by his schoolmaster and that as a young man he lost the woman he once loved. Alternatively, they may say that they have less sympathy for him because he was loved by his sister, liked by Fezziwig and Dick

Wilkins, and loved by a woman but chose to dedicate his life to amassing wealth instead of enjoying friendship and love.

Difficulty: *Average*
Objective: *Essay*

17. Students should recognize that Marley is saying that he had misunderstood his business. He now realizes that instead of enriching himself, he should have been working to improve humanity—by giving money to the poor, showing sympathy, having patience, and acting kindly. Students should justify this explanation by noting that Marley says that if people do not act in a positive manner during their lifetime, they are condemned to do so after they die—or, presumably, suffer consequences.

    Difficulty: *Challenging*
    Objective: *Essay*

18. Students should point out that in Scene 1, Marley describes Scrooge as "tightfisted," "grasping," and "solitary." In Scene 3, however, Marley tells Scrooge that he has a chance and a hope of escaping his own fate, so he sees that Scrooge still has some humanity within him.

    Difficulty: *Average*
    Objective: *Essay*

A Christmas Carol: Scrooge and Marley, *Act II*, by Israel Horovitz

Vocabulary Warm-up Exercises, p. 45

A.
1. recollect
2. poem
3. thoughtful
4. fortune
5. heartily
6. praise
7. unaltered
8. value

B. Sample Answers

1. T; A *beggar* is someone who asks for charity, which means he or she does not have enough money to live properly.
2. T; Stealing is against the law, and if one is caught stealing, there will be a bad *consequence*, or "result of an action," such as being arrested and going to jail.
3. F; *Preserved* means "saved," and if we threw out the photos we did not save them.
4. F; If Brenda likes the smell, she does not think it is *odious*, which means "disgusting."
5. T; Most people like to be told to do something in a polite way, and *nasty* means "unpleasant."
6. F; *Workhouses* are poorhouses, where poor people who could not pay their debts were sent.
7. T; A *refuge* is a safe place to go, and if we don't have one then we cannot escape the storm.

8. T; A *resource* is something we can draw upon if needed, and if we are doing a big office project, the extra paper may come in handy.

Reading Warm-up A, p. 46

Sample Answers

1. (his past); A synonym for *recollect* is *remember.*
2. in money; Scrooge does not have a *fortune* in good values or kindliness.
3. (Scrooge); A *poem* is "a written piece that presents a powerful image or feeling and uses rhythmic or rhyming words."
4. When he realizes that few will ever miss him because of the sort of life he has lived; She became very *thoughtful* after reading the moving story.
5. (change); I would like our tradition of eating turkey on Thanksgiving to remain *unaltered.*
6. He brings good humor to all and generosity to those in need. *Heartily* means "sincerely and fully."
7. sharing with others; I know the *value* of having my sister as a good friend.
8. (his generous actions); An antonym of *praise* is *criticize.*

Reading Warm-up B, p. 47

Sample Answers

1. the growth of more slums; *Consequence* means "a result of an action."
2. (because the government had no laws to protect them); The kindhearted woman gave some food to the *beggars.*
3. (unclean); A synonym for *odious* is *disgusting.*
4. This was because they could be paid lower wages than men. *Resource* means "something that can be drawn upon and used if needed."
5. the rights of children; The new law *preserved* the high standards for safe drinking water.
6. (the poor); *Workhouses* were different from the prisons because the poor were given jobs there to help provide them with food and shelter. In the prisons, they were treated as criminals and locked up with other kinds of criminals.
7. conditions in the workhouses; I think it is *nasty* to have to look through garbage when I have mistakenly thrown away something valuable.
8. (Many poor); *Refuge* means "a safe place or shelter from danger."

Writing About the Big Question, p. 48

A. 1. appearance
2. bias
3. focus

B. Sample Answers

1. People can communicate by telephone, talking face-to-face, or by sending email, letters or telegrams. People can also communicate by body language.

2. Email is an easy, convenient, and inexpensive way to communicate. It does have a few shortcomings, however. For example, it can be hard to **perceive** a person's tone by what they write. You may make the **assumption** that someone is joking when they are really quite serious.

C. Sample Answer

In order to change, we must first identify what it is we want to change. Talking to friends and family can help you learn about ways in which you can improve. These people know you best and are most aware of your good and bad points.

Reading: Adjust Your Reading Rate to Suit Your Purpose, p. 49

Sample Answers

1. I would read the dialogue quickly in order to create a feeling of conversation.
2. I would read the stage directions slowly and carefully, to look for information about action not revealed in the dialogue.
3. The stage directions reveal that the Ghost of Christmas Present sprinkles the two speakers with a substance. That action explains why the speakers suddenly treat each other respectfully.
4. I would read the passage slowly in order to reflect on the character's words and look for clues to the message.

Literary Analysis: Stage Directions, p. 50

1. Bob Cratchit and his son Tiny Tim
2. The "threadbare and fringeless comforter" indicates that the Cratchits are poor.
3. Tiny Tim wears leg braces and walks with the aid of crutches. He is light enough that his father easily bears him on his shoulders.
4. Scrooge and the Ghost of Christmas Future appear in this scene. The reader knows that Scrooge is there because he speaks. The reader knows that Christmas Future is there because his presence is announced in the stage directions.
5. The stage directions show that the setting changes. The Cratchits' home fades out, and a tombstone comes into view. Christmas Future points to the tombstone. Readers will therefore understand why Scrooge realizes at this moment that it was his own death that the businessmen, Old Joe, Mrs. Dilber, and the others were talking about.

Vocabulary Builder, p. 51

A. Sample answers follow each yes or no designation:

1. Yes, they will—*astonish* means "to amaze."
2. No, he cannot easily resist—a compulsion is an irresistible force.
3. No, she does not—*severe* means "harsh."
4. No, it was not—*meager* means "small in amount."

5. Yes, they can—*audible* means "loud enough to be heard."

6. Yes—to *intercede* means "to act on behalf of someone who is in trouble."

B. 1. My parents have frequently *interceded* on my behalf.

2. An *intercepted* ball does not reach its destination.

3. A highway *intersection* is a place where two roads meet.

Enrichment: Holiday Observances, p. 52

A. Students should name a holiday and accurately answer the questions about that holiday, describing its meaning, the clothing typically worn on the holiday, the foods typically eaten during its observance, any places visited during its observance, any activities engaged in, and any other traditions relating to it.

B. Students should name their made-up holiday, describe its purpose, and describe traditions to be associated with it.

Integrated Language Skills: Grammar, p. 53

A. 1. ✗
2. ✓
3. ✓
4. ✗
5. ✗

B. Sample Answers

1. We do not have any bread for sandwiches.

2. The spy never had any intention of giving himself up.

3. This article does not have anything to do with our assignment.

4. They are not going to any championship game tonight.

5. Our dog will not ever eat any food she does not like.

Open-Book Test, p. 56

Short Answer

1. The passage is set off in brackets and printed in italic type. It describes the costume of The Ghost of Christmas Present and the set that is the room in which Present appears.

   Difficulty: *Easy*   **Objective:** *Literary Analysis*

2. Scrooge invites the Ghost to teach him, which he never would have done before. He realizes that he has something to learn.

   Difficulty: *Easy*   **Objective:** *Interpretation*

3. Horovitz suggests that the director can decide what the chorus will sing. The directions indicate that the fact of them singing is more important than what they sing.

   Difficulty: *Challenging*   **Objective:** *Literary Analysis*

4. It should be read slowly because it is a longer speech and it contains an important message.

   Difficulty: *Easy*   **Objective:** *Reading*

5. It should be read quickly because it is a conversation, and so it should be read like two people talking.

   Difficulty: *Average*   **Objective:** *Reading*

6. Scrooge would have surprised his nephew and niece if he'd been heard, but he might have been able to join in happily.

   Difficulty: *Average*   **Objective:** *Vocabulary*

7. Scrooge means that the place frightened him and he wants to go, but he will not forget the lesson he learned there.

   Difficulty: *Average*   **Objective:** *Interpretation*

8. Scrooge means that he may have an opportunity to change the future in a positive way.

   Difficulty: *Average*   **Objective:** *Interpretation*

9. He acquired the traits of kindness and generosity, which are usually considered the important aspects of the Christmas spirit.

   Difficulty: *Challenging*   **Objective:** *Interpretation*

10. [col 2, row 2] The English rich eat very well, as opposed to the very poor people.

    [col 2, row 3] Tiny Tim is poor.

    [col 2, row 4] Scrooge has changed and now is able to show affection.

    Scrooge moves on the stage direction of [*Scrooge goes to him and embraces him.*]

    Difficulty: *Average*   **Objective:** *Literary Analysis*

Essay

11. Students should recognize that the Ghost of Christmas Future is frightening because he does not speak, he represents Scrooge's death, and he shows Scrooge the effects of his death on others.

    Difficulty: *Easy*   **Objective:** *Essay*

12. Students should describe Tiny Tim's leg braces and crutches. They may note that he is very small and light. They should refer to his musings at church and his selflessness. They might suggest that he is the focal point of his family and appears to represent goodness.

    Difficulty: *Average*   **Objective:** *Essay*

13. In response to the first message, students should cite the effect, that Scrooge's change has on the Cratchits, his nephew, and his community. In response to the second message, they should refer to the meeting of the three businessmen and to the people who divide up Scrooge's possessions after his death. In response to the third message, they should cite Scrooge's joy as he buys gifts on Christmas day, contributes to the poor, and raises Bob Cratchit's salary.

    Difficulty: *Challenging*   **Objective:** *Essay*

14. Students should note that Bob Cratchit sees Scrooge as a man who allows him to earn a living, while Mrs. Cratchit sees him as stingy and unfeeling. Fred pities him

and sees him as one who is both comical and tragic, while his wife has no patience with him. Students may feel that Fred sees Scrooge most clearly because he sees his uncle's potential as well as his present character.

Difficulty: *Average* **Objective:** *Essay*

Oral Response

15. Oral responses should be clear, well organized, and well supported by appropriate examples from the selection.

    Difficulty: *Average* **Objective:** *Oral Interpretation*

Selection Test A, p. 59

Critical Reading

1.	ANS: B	DIF: Easy	OBJ: Literary Analysis
2.	ANS: D	DIF: Easy	OBJ: Interpretation
3.	ANS: C	DIF: Easy	OBJ: Literary Analysis
4.	ANS: C	DIF: Easy	OBJ: Interpretation
5.	ANS: A	DIF: Easy	OBJ: Comprehension
6.	ANS: C	DIF: Easy	OBJ: Comprehension
7.	ANS: A	DIF: Easy	OBJ: Reading
8.	ANS: A	DIF: Easy	OBJ: Interpretation
9.	ANS: D	DIF: Easy	OBJ: Comprehension
10.	ANS: B	DIF: Easy	OBJ: Reading

Vocabulary and Grammar

11.	ANS: B	DIF: Easy	OBJ: Vocabulary
12.	ANS: D	DIF: Easy	OBJ: Grammar

Essay

13. Students should recognize that in both instances, Scrooge visits families that are happy but not wealthy. In both cases, too, the wife believes Scrooge is a miser, whereas the husband defends him. Scrooge learns that happiness is more important than wealth, and for the first time he seems to care what people think of him—and is disturbed to find out that he is not universally well thought of.

    Difficulty: *Easy*

    Objective: *Essay*

14. Students should recognize that the Ghost of Christmas Future is frightening because he does not speak and because he shows Scrooge disturbing scenes—people talking about Scrooge's death, people who have stolen Scrooge's belongings after his death, and Scrooge's own gravestone.

    Difficulty: *Easy*

    Objective: *Essay*

15. Students should note that Bob Cratchit sees Scrooge as a man who allows him to earn a living. Mrs. Cratchit sees him as stingy and unfeeling. Fred pities him, but his wife has no patience with him. Students may feel

that Fred sees Scrooge most clearly because he sees his uncle's potential as well as his present character.

Difficulty: *Average*

Objective: *Essay*

Selection Test B, p. 62

Critical Reading

1.	ANS: B	DIF: Challenging	OBJ: Interpretation
2.	ANS: C	DIF: Average	OBJ: Literary Analysis
3.	ANS: C	DIF: Challenging	OBJ: Literary Analysis
4.	ANS: B	DIF: Average	OBJ: Reading
5.	ANS: B	DIF: Average	OBJ: Literary Analysis
6.	ANS: C	DIF: Average	OBJ: Reading
7.	ANS: A	DIF: Average	OBJ: Comprehension
8.	ANS: C	DIF: Average	OBJ: Interpretation
9.	ANS: A	DIF: Average	OBJ: Interpretation
10.	ANS: D	DIF: Challenging	OBJ: Interpretation

Vocabulary and Grammar

11.	ANS: A	DIF: Average	OBJ: Vocabulary
12.	ANS: D	DIF: Challenging	OBJ: Vocabulary
13.	ANS: D	DIF: Challenging	OBJ: Grammar

Essay

14. In response to the first message, students should cite the effect that Scrooge's change has on the Cratchits, his nephew's family, and his community. In response to the second, they should refer to the meeting of the three businessmen and to the men and women who divide up Scrooge's possessions after his death. In response to the third message, they should cite Scrooge's giddiness as he buys gifts on Christmas Day, contributes to the poor, raises Bob Cratchit's salary, and so on.

    Difficulty: *Average*

    Objective: *Essay*

15. Students should describe Tiny Tim's leg braces and crutches. They might note that he is light enough to be carried by his father. They should refer to his musings at church and his selflessness. They might suggest that he is the focal point of his family and appears to represent goodness.

    Difficulty: *Average*

    Objective: *Essay*

16. Students should note that Bob Cratchit sees Scrooge as a man who allows him to earn a living, while Mrs. Cratchit sees him as stingy and unfeeling. Fred pities him and sees him as one who is both comical and tragic, while his wife has no patience with him. Students may feel that Fred sees Scrooge most clearly because he sees his uncle's potential as well as his present character.

    Difficulty: *Average*

    Objective: *Essay*

from A Christmas Carol: Scrooge and Marley,
Act I, Scenes 3 & 5 by Israel Horovitz

Vocabulary Warm-up Exercises, p. 66

A. 1. enormously
2. feast
3. suitors
4. compete
5. absolute
6. faintly
7. grace
8. gratitude

B. Sample Answers

1. No, *apprentices* usually receive room and board and instruction, not a salary, in return for working.

2. No, if it is *convenient* that means it is easily accomplished, so it would not take a long time.

3. Yes, if we are *bound* to run into a snowstorm, it means it will very likely happen, and therefore the trip may take longer than usual.

4. Yes, standing at *attention* means assuming a tall, standing posture and awaiting an order, which is a military custom.

5. No, most people like being treated with *dignity* because it means they are treated with respect and are held in high esteem.

6. No, if the person is a *master*, that means he or she is very skilled at the job or is the boss and probably knows a lot about the shop and the craft.

7. Yes, the room will probably grow darker because *snuffs* means "extinguishes," and when there is less light from a flame it gets darker in a room.

8. Yes, a person is likely to earn more *wages* by working more because wages are pay, and more pay is usually earned by working longer hours.

Reading Warm-up A, p. 67

Sample Answers

1. (holiday party); *Absolute* means "complete or whole."
2. Some dancers; When the runner sprinted, she ran with great *grace*.
3. (to see how many high kicks, fancy steps, and turns they could do); People may also *compete* in guessing games, soccer, or chess.
4. They stood by her side as they awaited a turn to dance with her. *Suitors* are "men who are courting a woman."
5. (goose and beef), (tasty treats); I enjoy a *feast* of pizza with extra garlic and a salad.
6. The tasty treats; Synonyms for *enormously* are *greatly* and *immensely*.
7. The entire family sang carols. The family's singing must have sounded loud and boisterous.
8. (for having such a fine family with whom to celebrate); *Gratitude* means "thankfulness."

Reading Warm-up B, p. 68

Sample Answers

1. cheap labor; *Bound* means "certain, sure, or having one's mind made up."

2. (to ask the workhouses to give them youngsters as apprentices); It is *convenient* to take a short cut to school because it makes the trip shorter.

3. (If a child became an apprentice, he or she would learn a trade, such as blacksmith or glass blower. The child would be given room and board in exchange for working for a master.) If I were an *apprentice*, I would like to learn how to make jewelry.

4. the owner or boss of the shop; One master was especially kind to his apprentices.

5. pay; I think it is unfair for anyone to be asked to work for no *wages*.

6. (treated the young workers with respect); *Dignity* means "the quality of being worthy of honor or respect."

7. ready to perform the next task required of them; Others who might stand at *attention* are military cadets.

8. (the youngsters' spirit was extinguished); *Snuffs* means "puts out or extinguishes a candle or something else."

Writing About the Big Question, p. 69

A. 1. assumption
2. reflect
3. reveal

B. Sample Answers

1. I am hard-working, red-headed, and plain spoken.

2. My pink cowboy boots **reveal** my usually hidden silly side. Most days, the **appearance** of my feet is practical. I wear gym shoes, snow boots, or flats. You will only see my pink cowboy boots at parties and special occasions. They completely change my **image**.

C. Sample Answer

Over time, people change the way they feel about their parents. As young children, we see our parents as all-powerful. By the time we are teenagers, we begin to understand that our parents have limitations. Once we become parents ourselves, we may judge those limitations with more understanding.

Literary Analysis: Comparing Characters, p. 70

Sample Answers

1. *Scrooge* complains that Cratchit will want to take off Christmas Day and that Cratchit is picking his pocket by getting paid for the day. He asks Cratchit not to wish him a merry Christmas. *Fezziwig* orders his apprentices to stop working because it is Christmas Eve. He announces that they will have a party, orders a fiddler to play, and calls for his daughters.

2. *Scrooge* only complains. *Fezziwig* arranges a party, to which he invites his employees, his family, his daughters'

"suitors," and others from the community; he laughs and dances.

3. *Scrooge* sees Christmas as an intrusion on his business. *Fezziwig* welcomes Christmas and celebrates it with generosity.

4. Cratchit indirectly reminds *Scrooge* that the next day is Christmas and teases him by wishing him a merry Christmas after Scrooge forbids him to do so. Dick Wilkins and the young Scrooge say that they are blessed to have a master like *Fezziwig*, and Scrooge promises that if he ever owns a business, he will treat his apprentices as well as Fezziwig treats them.

5. *Scrooge:* selfish, greedy, manipulative, mean; *Fezziwig:* happy, generous, kind

Vocabulary Builder, p. 71

A. Sample Answers

fiddler: Definition—person who plays a fiddle; *Synonym*—violinist; *Example sentence*—The fiddler played a waltz.

suitors: Definition—men who pay attention to women in the hopes of marrying them; *Synonyms*—beaus, boyfriends; *Example sentence*—The heiress had ten suitors, while her poor cousin had none.

Snuffs: Definition—puts out, as a candle; *Synonym*—extinguishes; *Example sentence*—My mother snuffs out candles with her fingers.

B. 1. C; 2. A; 3. D

Open-Book Test, p. 73

Short Answer

1. Cratchit extinguishes his candle as a cost-savings. He might also put out the candle as a safety measure to prevent a fire.
   Difficulty: *Easy*   **Objective:** *Vocabulary*

2. Cratchit knows he has made Scrooge angry by wishing him a merry Christmas when Scrooge warned him not to do it.
   Difficulty: *Easy*   **Objective:** *Interpretation*

3. Scrooge gets angry because he cares only about making money, and Christmas interrupts his business. This shows that he is greedy and selfish.
   Difficulty: *Average*   **Objective:** *Literary Analysis*

4. Fezziwig loves to celebrate Christmas. The fact that he brings in fiddlers, has everyone dancing, and provides piles of food shows his pleasure in the holiday.
   Difficulty: *Average*   **Objective:** *Interpretation*

5. The men have arrived to see Fezziwig's daughters because suitors are men who are courting women.
   Difficulty: *Average*   **Objective:** *Vocabulary*

6. Fezziwig is kind and generous to everyone, no matter what, while Scrooge is cold and harsh to everyone.
   Difficulty: *Challenging*   **Objective:** *Literary Analysis*

7. Young Ebenezer and Dick Wilkins admire Fezziwig very much because he is kind, generous, and good to his employees.
   Difficulty: *Easy*   **Objective:** *Literary Analysis*

8. Most students will say yes, it is surprising, because they have learned that when Scrooge has his own firm, he treats his employees harshly.
   Difficulty: *Challenging*   **Objective:** *Interpretation*

9. Fezziwig is shown as a kind, generous, fun-loving employer in Act I, Scene 5. This contrasts with Scrooge, who is shown as a mean-spirited, stingy employer in his relations with Cratchit in Act I, Scene 2.
   Difficulty: *Average*   **Objective:** *Literary Analysis*

10. Young Ebenezer: admiring of Fezziwig, idealistic, kind, respectful
    Bob Cratchit: humble, gentle
    Fezziwig: generous, kind, fun-loving
    Students might say that Cratchit's gentleness contrasts the most with the older Scrooge's brusque disdain for others; Fezziwig's generosity and fun-loving manner contrasts the most with Scrooge's stinginess and dour attitude; or Young Ebenezer's youthful idealism and respect contrasts the most with the older Scrooge's absence of faith in and respect for humanity.
    Difficulty: *Average*   **Objective:** *Literary Analysis*

Essay

11. Students should recognize that the two men are opposites as bosses: Scrooge is cheap and resentful, while Fezziwig is kind and generous. Students will probably state that they would prefer to work for Fezziwig. They should support their responses with details from the play.
    Difficulty: *Easy*   **Objective:** *Essay*

12. Students should cite details showing that Scrooge is greedy and unkind while Cratchit is patient, sympathetic, and kind. Most students will believe that Cratchit is the happier man, despite his lack of material wealth. Their responses to the question of which man is happier should be well reasoned.
    Difficulty: *Average*   **Objective:** *Essay*

13. Students should note that the younger Scrooge is happy, grateful, and friendly, while the older Scrooge is unhappy, ungrateful, and unfriendly. They should cite details from the scenes to support their responses.
    Difficulty: *Challenging*   **Objective:** *Essay*

14. Students should note that Scrooge sees his younger self as an open, grateful young man who is determined to do good. They may point out that seeing himself as he once was, and seeing Fezziwig as an example of a good employer, opened his eyes to the way he is as an older man, and led him to change his behavior.
    Difficulty: *Average*   **Objective:** *Essay*

Oral Response

15. Oral responses should be clear, well organized, and well supported by appropriate examples from the selection.

    Difficulty: *Average* **Objective:** *Oral Interpretation*

Selection Test A, p. 76

Critical Reading

1. ANS: B	DIF: Easy	OBJ: Comprehension
2. ANS: A	DIF: Easy	OBJ: Comprehension
3. ANS: D	DIF: Easy	OBJ: Comprehension
4. ANS: B	DIF: Easy	OBJ: Interpretation
5. ANS: B	DIF: Easy	OBJ: Literary Analysis
6. ANS: C	DIF: Easy	OBJ: Comprehension
7. ANS: D	DIF: Easy	OBJ: Comprehension
8. ANS: D	DIF: Easy	OBJ: Comprehension
9. ANS: D	DIF: Easy	OBJ: Interpretation
10. ANS: A	DIF: Easy	OBJ: Literary Analysis
11. ANS: C	DIF: Easy	OBJ: Literary Analysis
12. ANS: A	DIF: Easy	OBJ: Literary Analysis

Vocabulary

13. ANS: D	DIF: Easy	OBJ: Vocabulary
14. ANS: A	DIF: Easy	OBJ: Vocabulary
15. ANS: C	DIF: Easy	OBJ: Vocabulary

Essay

16. Students should recognize that Scrooge is not a nice or an understanding employer. They should note that he does not provide adequate heat, he pays Cratchit a meager salary, and he resents giving him one paid day off a year. Students should state whether they would want to work for Scrooge and support their explanation with a detail from the excerpt.

    Difficulty: *Easy*

    Objective: *Essay*

17. Students should recognize that Fezziwig is Scrooge's opposite: He is kind and generous to his employees; he invites his employees, his servants, his family, his daughters' suitors—virtually everyone—to a Christmas party; he is fair and understanding. His apprentices appreciate and admire him. Students should state whether they would want to work for someone like Fezziwig and support their explanation with two details from the excerpt.

    Difficulty: *Easy*

    Objective: *Essay*

18. Students should note that Scrooge sees his younger self as an open, grateful young man who wants to do good. They may point out that seeing himself as he once was

opens his eyes to the way he is as an older man and leads him to change his behavior.

Difficulty: *Average*

Objective: *Essay*

Selection Test B, p. 79

Critical Reading

1. ANS: C	DIF: Average	OBJ: Comprehension
2. ANS: C	DIF: Average	OBJ: Comprehension
3. ANS: B	DIF: Average	OBJ: Interpretation
4. ANS: D	DIF: Average	OBJ: Interpretation
5. ANS: C	DIF: Average	OBJ: Literary Analysis
6. ANS: D	DIF: Average	OBJ: Comprehension
7. ANS: D	DIF: Average	OBJ: Comprehension
8. ANS: B	DIF: Average	OBJ: Interpretation
9. ANS: D	DIF: Average	OBJ: Interpretation
10. ANS: A	DIF: Average	OBJ: Interpretation
11. ANS: D	DIF: Challenging	OBJ: Literary Analysis
12. ANS: D	DIF: Average	OBJ: Literary Analysis
13. ANS: A	DIF: Challenging	OBJ: Literary Analysis
14. ANS: B	DIF: Average	OBJ: Literary Analysis

Vocabulary

15. ANS: B	DIF: Average	OBJ: Vocabulary
16. ANS: B	DIF: Average	OBJ: Vocabulary
17. ANS: A	DIF: Average	OBJ: Vocabulary

Essay

18. Students should cite details showing that Scrooge is greedy and unkind while Cratchit is patient, sympathetic, and kind, and they should write a lucid, well-reasoned response to the question of which man they think would make the better boss.

    Difficulty: *Average*

    Objective: *Essay*

19. Students should note that the young Scrooge is happy, grateful, and friendly, whereas the older Scrooge is unhappy, ungrateful, and unfriendly; they should cite at least one detail from each scene to support their arguments.

    Difficulty: *Challenging*

    Objective: *Essay*

20. Students should note that Scrooge sees his younger self as an open, grateful young man who is determined to do good. They may point out that seeing himself as he once was, and seeing Fezziwig as an example of a good employer, opened his eyes to the way he is as an older man and led him to change his behavior.

    Difficulty: *Average*

    Objective: *Essay*

Writing Workshop

Multimedia Report: Integrating Grammar Skills, p. 83

A. 1. beside; 2. except; 3. into; 4. advice; 5. effect

B. 1. correct
2. I would advise you to go into the house before it rains.
3. Many people besides me accept my mother's advice.

Benchmark Test 9, p. 84

MULTIPLE CHOICE

1. ANS: B
2. ANS: A
3. ANS: D
4. ANS: D
5. ANS: C
6. ANS: A
7. ANS: B
8. ANS: A
9. ANS: A
10. ANS: D
11. ANS: A
12. ANS: B
13. ANS: C
14. ANS: B
15. ANS: C
16. ANS: A
17. ANS: D
18. ANS: C
19. ANS: B
20. ANS: B
21. ANS: C
22. ANS: A
23. ANS: C
24. ANS: B
25. ANS: C
26. ANS: C
27. ANS: D
28. ANS: A
29. ANS: C
30. ANS: A
31. ANS: D
32. ANS: B
33. ANS: D

ESSAY

34. Students' letters should express an opinion for or against the topic. They should include at least two main points, with supporting details. Each letter should include a salutation and a signature.

35. Students' tributes should be brief and should clearly state the qualities they admire in the people they write about. Each tribute should end with a concluding statement.

36. Students' paragraphs should express a clear topic for the report, with a description of the organizational plan and the types of media that will be used. Students should also describe the effects they hope to achieve with the various media.

"The Monsters Are Due on Maple Street"
by Rod Serling

Vocabulary Warm-up Exercises, p. 92

A. 1. afford
2. broadcast
3. hesitant
4. process
5. typical
6. Gradually
7. mildly
8. Obviously

B. Sample Answers

1. T; Few people have been able to reach the summit of Mount Everest, so it is an enormous, or *tremendous*, accomplishment indeed.

2. F; It wouldn't be fun to go camping in an area that is full of streets and homes.

3. F; You can never replace something that is *unique* because it is one of a kind.

4. F; It's not always fun to be around an *intense* person because he or she takes everything too seriously.

5. F; When you are in a hurry, you are too distracted to be thoughtful and to think about things in a *reflective* way.

6. T; Dreams are a different level of consciousness beyond normal time and space, so you are in a different *dimension*.

7. T; If a horror movie is good, it will both scare and surprise the audience, so the *reaction* would be to scream with fright.

8. F; *Prejudices* are caused by fear and misinformation, so if a person gets over his or her fear and becomes informed, he or she can overcome prejudices.

Reading Warm-up A, p. 93

Sample Answers

1. (televisions); *Afford* means "having enough money to buy something"
2. a big wooden box with a tiny 10-inch or 15-inch video screen; A *typical* TV set today has a flat screen measuring 25 to 50 inches wide. It can be free-standing or propped up on the wall.
3. (shows); Unfortunately, the shows were only slightly entertaining.
4. the screens got bigger. The picture improved, and so did the shows; Through practice, I am *gradually* becoming a better athlete.
5. the situation comedy, or "sitcom"; My favorite kind of *broadcast* is the reality show.
6. discontinuing black-and-white TVs and introducing color; I am in the *process* of completing my vocabulary assignment.
7. (eager); *Hesitant* means "unwilling to do something because you are unsure about it."
8. an unreal picture of real America; *Clearly*, TV changed people's lives.

Reading Warm-up B, p. 94

Sample Answers

1. There was no other show like it; Rod Serling was a writer with a *unique* voice.
2. lined with modest houses; A *residential* street in my area has old houses with great big yards and fences.
3. between dreams and imagination; They entered a *world* between dreams and imagination.
4. (thoughtful); I am usually feeling *reflective* at night when I lie awake thinking.
5. (introduction); My friend Jackie is an *intense* person who gets seriously involved in things that are important to her.
6. ideas and other people; People's *prejudices* against other people cause a lot of unhappiness.
7. (his shows), other TV shows of the time; A synonym for *tremendous* is *huge.*
8. audiences were ready for more thoughtful programs; *Reaction* means, "an action or feeling that is a response to something."

Writing About the Big Question, p. 95

A. 1. characteristic
2. identify
3. ignore

B. Sample Answers

1. with their clothing, with their attitude toward school, by the friends they choose, by how friendly they are to others, etc.
2. I think school uniforms are a good idea. Without uniforms, kids think too much about their appearance. They lose **focus** on their schoolwork. When all of the kids wear the same thing, kids are forced to **reveal** their personalities in ways that are more meaningful than what they are wearing.

Reading: Distinguish Between Important and Unimportant Details to Write a Summary, p. 96

1. An out-of-the-ordinary event occurs, no one can explain it satisfactorily, and a boy starts talking about aliens.
2. The unnecessary detail is that Tommy wears eyeglasses.
3. The neighbors become suspicious of Les Goodman, and he says that they are letting a nightmare begin.
4. The unnecessary detail is that Goodman compares the neighbors to frightened rabbits. It is clear that it is unimportant because it is not necessary to an understanding of the play; the play would be complete and forceful without it.

Literary Analysis: A Character's Motives, p. 97

1. Steve may be motivated by confusion, fear, and a desire to find a reasonable explanation for the seemingly mysterious events.
2. Goodman
3. Don
4. anger and/or fear
5. Goodman is angry because his neighbors are acting as if he were responsible for the strange events. He may be frightened because he realizes that they are acting irrationally.

Vocabulary Builder, p. 98

A. Sample answers follow each yes or no designation:

1. No; a flustered person is nervous and so would not be likely to speak clearly.
2. No; a river would move quickly after a heavy rain.
3. Yes; someone who asks the same question firmly and steadily must be eager to know the answer.
4. Yes; a child who is boldly resisting would be likely to refuse to do his chores.
5. No; if the person has undergone a change, she is not likely to continue to be the way she used to be.
6. Yes—*transfixed* means "held motionless with amazement" so the person would be interested.

B. 1. An *assistant* is a person who helps you, not someone who competes with you.
2. If you *insist* on doing something, you are expressing yourself in a firm manner.
3. A *persistent* person will not give up easily.

Enrichment: Script Writing, p. 99

Students should describe a setting, two or more characters, and a science-fiction plot, including the conflict, the resolution, and a lesson that is conveyed by one of the characters.

Integrated Language Skills: Grammar, p. 100

A. 1. ? interrogative
2. . declarative
3. ! exclamatory
4. . declarative
5. . *or* ! imperative
6. . declarative
7. ? interrogative

B. Students' dialogues should include all four kinds of sentences, with each sentence correctly identified.

Open-Book Test, p. 103

Short Answer

1. The people get confused, nervous, and upset because the power goes out with no explanation.
   Difficulty: *Easy*   **Objective:** *Vocabulary*

2. Steve wants to reassure himself, and the others, that there is a logical explanation and nothing to fear.
   Difficulty: *Easy*   **Objective:** *Literary Analysis*

3. Tommy says that aliens resembling humans are sent ahead to prepare for a landing. The neighbors begin to think that one of them could be an alien. They begin to think that way as they become more fearful.
   Difficulty: *Average*   **Objective:** *Interpretation*

4. A flash of light occurs, and the power goes off on Maple Street. The neighbors gather, and as they speak together, they become nervous and suspicious of one another.
   Difficulty: *Easy*   **Objective:** *Reading*

5. The detail shows that the neighbors' mistrust of one another has grown to huge proportions. They are frightened enough to become violent.
   Difficulty: *Average*   **Objective:** *Reading*

6. They are motivated by suspicion and fear. They are beginning to wonder which of them might not be human.
   Difficulty: *Challenging*   **Objective:** *Literary Analysis*

7. The events on Maple Street have shown that people easily become suspicious, then fearful, then violent. The people on Maple Street were perfectly ordinary, so a similar situation could probably happen anywhere.
   Difficulty: *Challenging*   **Objective:** *Interpretation*

8. [col 1, row 2] Steve wants to calm people down and find out the truth.
   [col 1, row 3] Sally is suspicious and wants to find someone to blame.
   [col 1, row 4] Charlie is terrified.
   Steve: He wants the truth. Sally: She wants someone to blame.
   Difficulty: *Average*   **Objective:** *Literary Analysis*

9. The people of Maple Street change from a group of neighbors into an angry mob.
   Difficulty: *Average*   **Objective:** *Vocabulary*

10. The monsters are already there. They are the people, the characters in the play, who end up behaving like monsters in a horror movie because of fear and suspicion.
    Difficulty: *Easy*   **Objective:** *Interpretation*

Essay

11. Students should recognize that Steve's comment is meant to be humorous, so he is trying to amuse his neighbors to ease the tension. Students may also point out that Steve is frightened by the events and may think there is some truth in Tommy's comment about aliens.
    Difficulty: *Easy*   **Objective:** *Essay*

12. Students should describe their initial ideas about the causes of the mysterious events, and then explain what they thought when they discovered at the end of the play that the Figures seem to have been responsible. Students should give logical reasons for choosing to depict the Figures as they did.
    Difficulty: *Average*   **Objective:** *Essay*

13. Students should define *mob mentality* as "the way a group acts when fear causes them act together in an irrational manner." Students may note that the neighbors on Maple Street seem normal until they come together and experience fear. Students should point out that fear and suspicion may lead people to become hostile, angry, and violent.
    Difficulty: *Challenging*   **Objective:** *Essay*

14. Students should note that as the play progresses, the neighbors become more frightened, which leads to suspicion. As they search for explanations that do not exist, they begin seeing things that are not there and not seeing what is there.
    Difficulty: *Average*   **Objective:** *Essay*

Oral Response

15. Oral responses should be clear, well organized, and well supported by appropriate examples from the selection.
    Difficulty: *Average*   **Objective:** *Oral Interpretation*

Selection Test A, p. 106

Critical Reading

1. ANS: C	DIF: Easy	OBJ: Comprehension
2. ANS: B	DIF: Easy	OBJ: Literary Analysis
3. ANS: A	DIF: Easy	OBJ: Comprehension
4. ANS: B	DIF: Easy	OBJ: Literary Analysis
5. ANS: D	DIF: Easy	OBJ: Interpretation
6. ANS: A	DIF: Easy	OBJ: Reading
7. ANS: C	DIF: Easy	OBJ: Reading
8. ANS: C	DIF: Easy	OBJ: Interpretation
9. ANS: A	DIF: Easy	OBJ: Literary Analysis
10. ANS: A	DIF: Easy	OBJ: Interpretation

Vocabulary and Grammar

11. ANS: C   DIF: Easy   OBJ: Vocabulary
12. ANS: A   DIF: Easy   OBJ: Grammar

Essay

13. Students should recognize that Steve's comment is humorous, at least on the surface, so he is trying to amuse the neighbors, to ease the tension. They may also point out that like his neighbors, Steve is frightened by the inexplicable events and to some extent he may think there is some truth in Tommy's explanation. Therefore, he may also be motivated by a belief in the possibility of a visit by creatures from outer space.

    Difficulty: *Easy*

    Objective: *Essay*

14. Students should present a well-reasoned explanation of their choice. Those who choose to depict the characters as aliens should allude to the references at the end of the play that suggest that the creatures are indeed aliens. Those who choose to depict them as monsters should refer to the title of the play. Those who choose to depict them as human beings should refer to the message of the play: that we are all capable of being monsters.

    Difficulty: *Easy*

    Objective: *Essay*

15. Students should note that the neighbors become more frightened, which leads to suspicion. As they search for explanations that do not exist, they begin seeing things that aren't there and not seeing what is there.

    Difficulty: *Average*

    Objective: *Essay*

Selection Test B, p. 109

Critical Reading

1. ANS: B   DIF: Challenging   OBJ: Comprehension
2. ANS: C   DIF: Average   OBJ: Literary Analysis
3. ANS: B   DIF: Average   OBJ: Interpretation
4. ANS: C   DIF: Average   OBJ: Reading
5. ANS: B   DIF: Average   OBJ: Literary Analysis
6. ANS: D   DIF: Average   OBJ: Reading
7. ANS: B   DIF: Challenging   OBJ: Interpretation
8. ANS: C   DIF: Challenging   OBJ: Reading
9. ANS: A   DIF: Average   OBJ: Literary Analysis
10. ANS: A   DIF: Challenging   OBJ: Interpretation
11. ANS: A   DIF: Challenging   OBJ: Interpretation
12. ANS: D   DIF: Average   OBJ: Interpretation

Vocabulary and Grammar

13. ANS: A   DIF: Average   OBJ: Vocabulary
14. ANS: D   DIF: Challenging   OBJ: Vocabulary
15. ANS: C   DIF: Challenging   OBJ: Grammar

Essay

16. Students should recognize that fear has taken over the town and no one is thinking rationally; everyone is reacting emotionally. Charlie accuses Tommy to redirect the crowd's anger, which had been focused on him. The neighbors are ready to believe Charlie because Tommy was the one who had told them about the aliens' methods. Especially perceptive students may recognize that the neighbors willingly believe Charlie because he has not accused any of them.

    Difficulty: *Average*

    Objective: *Essay*

17. Students should coherently describe their initial ideas about the cause of the mysterious events and then describe what they thought when they discovered at the end of the play that aliens seem to have been responsible for the events.

    Difficulty: *Average*

    Objective: *Essay*

18. Students should note that as the play progresses, the neighbors become more frightened, which leads to suspicion. As they search for explanations that do not exist, they begin seeing things that aren't there and not seeing what is there.

    Difficulty: *Average*

    Objective: *Essay*

from Grandpa and the Statue by Arthur Miller
"My Head Is Full of Starshine" by Peg Kehret

Vocabulary Warm-up Exercises, p. 113

A.
1. decent
2. fines
3. notices (also accept *items*)
4. items (also accept *notices*)
5. announced
6. fund
7. contribute
8. appetite

B. Sample Answers

1. I will ask for my friend's help. If the help is *critical*, then my plan will not succeed without it.
2. If I find chess *fascinating*, I am very interested in it and will enjoy watching a game.
3. If I am looking *frantically* for my keys, then I am looking for them wildly or in a panic. I am not looking calmly.
4. No, new *immigrants* have not lived here all their lives. *Immigrants* are people who have arrived in a country from another place.
5. If someone is *stranded* in the woods, he or she should call for help on a cellphone so rescuers know where to find him or her.

6. If I found out the deal was a *swindle*, I would not take it. I might tell the police.

7. Buildings that *topple* in the wind are not well built. A well-built building would not fall over.

Reading Warm-up A, p. 114

Sample Answers

1. money; A *fund* is a collection of money for a specific purpose.

2. (give); I would like to *contribute* to the cause of cleaning up the environment.

3. she had already thought of a name; No, she did not keep it a secret. I know because *announced* means "told everyone."

4. ("To-do" List); Two other *items* that might also appear on the list are "choose a name for the club" and "decide how to get members."

5. food; The pizza parlor in my neighborhood serves *decent* food.

6. (talking); Exercising, especially swimming, gives me an *appetite*.

7. for overdue books; Other kinds of *fines* include parking fines.

8. (telling people when and where to go for the first meeting); I would write the words *Join a New Club* in the biggest letters.

Reading Warm-up B, p. 115

Sample Answers

1. in their desperation; Working slowly and calmly is the opposite of working *frantically*.

2. (If they run out of ideas); A drum is *hollow*.

3. in the middle of the story; *Stranded* means "stuck someplace without a way back."

4. (come crashing to the ground); To make sure something does not *topple*, you need to make sure it balances well and has a strong base.

5. where the story is headed; A filling lunch is *critical* in my day.

6. (moving to a new country); To become *immigrants*, people leave one country and move to a new one.

7. hard to put down; I think car engines are *fascinating*.

8. (cheated); A person who is smart and alert will not become the victim of a *swindle*.

Writing About the Big Question, p. 116

A. 1. image
2. perspective
3. perception

B. Sample Answers

1. People may get the wrong impression of another person based on a racial bias. People may get the wrong

impression of person who is the opposite sex. People may get the wrong impression of another person because they are from another culture, and behave differently.

2. I don't think I'd want to see myself as others do. I think it is healthy to believe we are putting our best **characteristics** forward. I'm afraid that seeing myself as others do would **reveal** some character flaws that would be impossible to change. It is best not to **focus** on things you cannot change.

C. Sample Answer

The best way to understand a person is to ask them about their dreams for the future. You may think you understand someone based on how they appear today. However, that person may be planning a very different future for themselves.

Literary Analysis: Comparing Dramatic Speeches, p. 117

Sample Answers

1. They learn that he is difficult to convince, distrustful, and doesn't like to spend his money.

2. The conflict is between Sheean, who wants Monaghan to give money for the Statue of Liberty's base, and Monaghan, who does not want to give the money.

3. His speech reveals that he was robbed when he first came to America, which has caused him to be suspicious and overly cautious.

4. The writer tells the reader that her teacher says she daydreams. She also says, "I pretend my chair is a flying carpet."

5. She seems to care about them a bit, but she also values her ability to be creative and would not trade it for being more organized.

Vocabulary Builder, p. 118

A. Sample Answers

1. Yes; if I accidentally threw away a diamond ring, I would likely be found searching through the trash.

2. No; a practical person would not ordinarily daydream and procrastinate.

3. No; someone who is relaxed and easygoing doesn't get annoyed, or peeved very easily.

4. Yes; someone who shows himself or herself to have the capability of being a great athlete may compete in the Olympics someday.

B. 1. D; 2. B; 3. C; 4. A

Open-Book Test, p. 120

Short Answer

1. Monaghan means he does not really want to discuss the matter. He is trying to change the subject.

Difficulty: *Challenging* **Objective:** *Interpretation*

2. It tells you that Sheean is easily impressed, and wants to impress others, since he thinks Roman numerals are high class.
   Difficulty: *Average*   **Objective:** *Literary Analysis*

3. Monaghan thinks Roman numerals and the date are too complicated, and the statue's message should be simple and easy to understand.
   Difficulty: *Easy*   **Objective:** *Interpretation*

4. Monaghan's speech reveals that because he was robbed when he was a newcomer to the country, he is very suspicious and does not trust or easily like people.
   Difficulty: *Challenging*   **Objective:** *Literary Analysis*

5. Her description of Pam reveals a lot about the speaker. Discussing Pam's differences tells what the speaker is like herself.
   Difficulty: *Average*   **Objective:** *Literary Analysis*

6. The science teacher would prefer Pam because she is the better student, pays attention, and finds science lessons fascinating.
   Difficulty: *Average*   **Objective:** *Interpretation*

7. The speaker in the monologue knows and accepts that she is disorganized and an imaginative daydreamer. Monaghan is not a daydreamer; he is super practical.
   Difficulty: *Easy*   **Objective:** *Literary Analysis*

8. Pam accepts the speaker as a friend even though they are very different. No, Sheean loses patience with Monaghan and probably wishes Monaghan were smarter and less stubborn.
   Difficulty: *Average*   **Objective:** *Interpretation*

9. No. Although the speaker is smart and has the capability to do well, she does not excel in science.
   Difficulty: *Average*   **Objective:** *Vocabulary*

10. [col 2, row 2] cheap, suspicious
    [col 2, row 3] patriotic, generous
    [col 2, row 4] creative, imaginative
    Students' choice of an admirable character should be reasonably supported.
    Difficulty: *Average*   **Objective:** *Literary Analysis*

Essay

11. Students should define a monologue as a speech by a single character that reveals thoughts and feelings, and a dialogue as a conversation between or among characters. *Grandpa and the Statue* is a dialogue because it is a conversation between two characters that reveals their traits. "My Head Is Full of Starshine" is a monologue because it is a speech by one character that reveals private thoughts and feelings.
    Difficulty: *Easy*   **Objective:** *Essay*

12. Students should recognize that Monaghan gives his speech to explain his experiences as a new immigrant. The speech reveals why Monaghan is so suspicious and unwilling to trust. The speaker of "My Head Is Full of Starshine" compares Pam to herself to point out their

differences. The speech reveals that the speaker knows she is forgetful and impractical, but also creative.
    Difficulty: *Average*   **Objective:** *Essay*

13. Students should recognize that the conflict between Monaghan and Sheean has to do with Monaghan's suspicious nature and Sheean's insistent personality. The conflict is resolved when Sheean decides to give the money himself. Students should recognize that the conflict between the speaker and Pam also has to do with the characters' differences. It is resolved at the end when the speaker announces that she is happy with herself as she is. Students should state which relationship they found more interesting and offer support for their opinion.
    Difficulty: *Challenging*   **Objective:** *Essay*

14. *Grandpa and the Statue:* Monaghan sees himself as clever and informed, but Sheean sees him more clearly as someone whose experiences have made him suspicious and cautious. "My Head Is Full of Starshine": Pam doesn't always understand her friend, but she sees her as creative and imaginative and values those traits.
    Difficulty: *Average*   **Objective:** *Essay*

Oral Response

15. Oral responses should be clear, well organized, and well supported by appropriate examples from the selections.
    Difficulty: *Average*   **Objective:** *Oral Interpretation*

Selection Test A, p. 123

Critical Reading

1. ANS: B	DIF: Easy	OBJ: Comprehension
2. ANS: C	DIF: Easy	OBJ: Literary Analysis
3. ANS: D	DIF: Easy	OBJ: Comprehension
4. ANS: A	DIF: Easy	OBJ: Comprehension
5. ANS: A	DIF: Easy	OBJ: Interpretation
6. ANS: B	DIF: Easy	OBJ: Interpretation
7. ANS: A	DIF: Easy	OBJ: Literary Analysis
8. ANS: B	DIF: Easy	OBJ: Comprehension
9. ANS: C	DIF: Easy	OBJ: Comprehension
10. ANS: A	DIF: Easy	OBJ: Literary Analysis
11. ANS: D	DIF: Easy	OBJ: Literary Analysis

Vocabulary

12. ANS: B	DIF: Easy	OBJ: Vocabulary
13. ANS: D	DIF: Easy	OBJ: Vocabulary
14. ANS: C	DIF: Easy	OBJ: Vocabulary

Essay

15. Students should recognize that Monaghan is giving his speech to explain his own experiences as a new immigrant. The speech reveals why Monaghan is so suspicious and unwilling to trust: He was robbed when he first came to America. The speaker of "My Head Is

Full of Starshine" compares Pam to herself to point out their differences. The speech reveals that the speaker knows she is forgetful and impractical but creative.

Difficulty: *Easy*

Objective: *Essay*

16. Students should explain that the excerpt from *Grandpa and the Statue* is a dialogue because it is a conversation between characters and "My Head Is Full of Starshine" is a monologue because it is a long, uninterrupted speech by one character. Students should state which character they prefer and explain their reasons.

Difficulty: *Easy*

Objective: *Essay*

17. *Grandpa and the Statue:* Monaghan sees himself as clever and informed, but Sheean sees him as suspicious and cautious. "My Head Is Full of Starshine": Pam doesn't always understand her friend, but she sees her as creative and imaginative and values those traits.

Difficulty: *Average*

Objective: *Essay*

Selection Test B, p. 126

Critical Reading

1. ANS: C	DIF: Average	OBJ: Literary Analysis
2. ANS: A	DIF: Challenging	OBJ: Interpretation
3. ANS: C	DIF: Challenging	OBJ: Literary Analysis
4. ANS: D	DIF: Challenging	OBJ: Comprehension
5. ANS: C	DIF: Average	OBJ: Interpretation
6. ANS: C	DIF: Average	OBJ: Literary Analysis
7. ANS: D	DIF: Challenging	OBJ: Literary Analysis
8. ANS: A	DIF: Average	OBJ: Comprehension
9. ANS: D	DIF: Average	OBJ: Interpretation
10. ANS: B	DIF: Average	OBJ: Comprehension
11. ANS: D	DIF: Average	OBJ: Interpretation
12. ANS: B	DIF: Average	OBJ: Literary Analysis
13. ANS: C	DIF: Average	OBJ: Literary Analysis
14. ANS: A	DIF: Challenging	OBJ: Literary Analysis

Vocabulary and Grammar

15. ANS: B	DIF: Average	OBJ: Vocabulary
16. ANS: B	DIF: Average	OBJ: Vocabulary
17. ANS: D	DIF: Average	OBJ: Vocabulary

Essay

18. Students should define monologues and dialogues according to the definitions in their textbooks and should correctly identify each selection. They might say that the excerpt from *Grandpa and the Statue* is a dialogue because it is a conversation between two characters and because the conversation reveals Monaghan's and Sheean's traits. They might say that "My Head Is Full of Starshine" is a monologue because it is a long,

uninterrupted speech by one character and it reveals her private thoughts and feelings.

Difficulty: *Average*

Objective: *Essay*

19. Students should recognize that the conflict between Monaghan and Sheean has to do with Monaghan's suspicious nature and Sheean's insistent personality. The conflict is resolved when Sheean gives up on convincing Monaghan to give money and gives it himself. Students should recognize that the conflict between the speaker in "My Head Is Full of Starshine" and Pam also has to do with the characters' differences. The conflict is resolved for the speaker only at the end, when she announces that she is largely happy with herself as she is. Students should state which relationship they found more interesting and offer a well-supported explanation for their opinion.

Difficulty: *Challenging*

Objective: *Essay*

20. *Grandpa and the Statue:* Monaghan sees himself as clever and informed, but Sheean sees him more clearly as someone whose experiences have made him suspicious and cautious. "My Head Is Full of Starshine": Pam doesn't always understand her friend, but she sees her as creative and imaginative and values those traits.

Difficulty: *Average*

Objective: *Essay*

Writing Workshop

Cause-and-Effect Essay: Integrating Grammar Skills, p. 130

A. 1. combine; 2. sell; 3. like; 4. produces; 5. is

B. 1. Milk and cheese often come from Wisconsin and Vermont.

2. Neither Wisconsin nor Vermont produces as much beef as Texas.

3. Either Brazil or Argentina is known for beef.

4. Neither Australia nor the British Isles have as many cows as Canada.

Vocabulary Workshop—1, p. 131

Sample Answers

A. 1. Sanskrit, Hindi; a discipline for achieving peace of mind through postures and concentration

2. Yiddish; a hard bread roll, shaped like a donut

3. Dutch; a whirlpool

4. American Indian; a black-and-white animal who emits a foul smell as a defense

5. Italian; a deep, purplish pink

6. Spanish; quickly

7. West African; a musical instrument played by strumming

8. French; a moving mass of loosened snow falling rapidly down an incline

B. 1. J. G. Zinn (1727–1759), German botanist; a colorful daisy-like flower

2. Captain C. C. Boycott, Irish land agent shunned by his neighbors; to refuse to buy, sell, or use in order to make a protest

3. V. Quisling (1887–1945), Norwegian politician who betrayed his country and helped the Nazis during World War II; a traitor

4. Adonis, Greek god, son of Aphrodite; a handsome man

5. Marie Curie (1867–1934), Polish chemist and physicist; a unit used to measure radioactivity

6. Madeleine Paulnier, a 19th-century French cook; a small, rich cake baked in a shell-shaped mold

7. Albert Einstein (1879–1955), American physicist, born in Germany; a radioactive chemical element

8. Queen Charlotte, wife of George III; a molded dessert made with strips of cake or bread and filled with custard

9. John L. McAdam (1756–1836), a Scot engineer; small stones bound together with tar to use as the surface of a road

10. Louis Pasteur (1822–1895), French chemist and bacteriologist; to heat milk in order to destroy bacteria

Benchmark Test 10, p. 134

MULTIPLE CHOICE

1. ANS: B
2. ANS: C
3. ANS: D
4. ANS: A
5. ANS: B
6. ANS: B
7. ANS: A
8. ANS: D
9. ANS: B
10. ANS: B
11. ANS: D
12. ANS: D
13. ANS: B
14. ANS: B
15. ANS: A
16. ANS: D
17. ANS: A
18. ANS: B
19. ANS: D
20. ANS: B
21. ANS: C
22. ANS: B
23. ANS: D
24. ANS: A
25. ANS: B
26. ANS: B
27. ANS: D
28. ANS: C
29. ANS: B
30. ANS: B
31. ANS: C
32. ANS: A
33. ANS: B

ESSAY

34. Students' paragraphs should describe a plan for writing a report. The paragraphs should include a plan for gathering information, an organizational plan, and at least two recommended changes for improving their neighborhood.

35. Students should choose one among several possible topics for a cause-and-effect essay. They should then write a sentence in which they tell why the topic interests them. Finally, they should list at least three questions related to the topic and to the type of essay.

36. Students' topic webs should show one main topic in a center circle, with at least four ideas or questions radiating from the main topic in additional circles that are connected to the main circle by lines. All of the ideas or questions should be related to the main topic.

Vocabulary in Context 5, p. 140

MULTIPLE CHOICE

1. ANS: D
2. ANS: A
3. ANS: C
4. ANS: D
5. ANS: B
6. ANS: C
7. ANS: C
8. ANS: B
9. ANS: D
10. ANS: B
11. ANS: D
12. ANS: C
13. ANS: B
14. ANS: C
15. ANS: A
16. ANS: C
17. ANS: C
18. ANS: A
19. ANS: B
20. ANS: D